GRINNING & GRINDING:

A COLLECTION OF
AMERICA'S DENTAL HUMOR

Volume 1

J.J. Portera

ISBN: 1-886049-02-5

Printed in the United States of America

Dental Humor by Dr. Joe Portera
13 Northtown, Suite 230
Jackson, MS 39211
601/957-2131
601/856-6461

If you would like to contribute a humorous dental story for Volume
II, send to Dr. Portera's address or FAX to him at 1-601-957-3772.

Book design and layout by Lori Leath-Smith

Published by: Best of Times, Inc.
P.O. Box 1360
Pelham, AL 35124

Price: $12.95
To obtain a copy of this book write to the above address.

This book is dedicated to *all* dentists, with a special sense of appreciation to those who strive, steadfastly, to search for the humor not always readily seen in a profession which is loaded to the gills with stress.

Their *grinning*, while bellied up to the chair in the daily *grinding* of dentistry, speaks of a special gift...to be saluted, and shared!

ACKNOWLEDGEMENTS

I thank Kathryn Rose, Caroline Lorraine, and Johanna Haley...three of the loveliest daughters a man could ever hope to have...for their patience while I wrote the book.

Patience so difficult, almost impossible, for an eleven, nine, and five year old to exercise, especially when they "love just being near Poppa."

I thank Susie, my wife and greatest fan, for *everything!* The least not being her own patience in living and loving a "perfectionist"!

I thank Kveta, my office receptionist, for endless hours of folding, addressing, and mailing the letters of solicitation to my colleagues around the country.

I thank Jim and Steve of The Best of Times, Inc., my publishers, for their confidence, support, and guidance.

I thank Leslie and Kathy of Seacoast Publishing for their editing, book layout and design, and, most of all, for their leading me to Brian Brasher, the best illustrationist I could have ever found. His pen and ink interpretations of my stories are so good, I accused him of being present at the scene of each of the events he so accurately conveys to the reader's visual imagination.

I thank Barry Hannah, "the best fiction writer in the South since Flannery O'Connor," as Larry McMurty once described him. Barry read the manuscript when it was naked as a jay-bird! He took the time from his own writing and academic duties at the University of Mississippi to read the unedited and non-illustrated stories.

I thank my mother and father, John and Rose, for their lifetime of loving, encouraging, and supporting me in each and every one of my endeavors, especially my creative enthusiasms.

Finally, but not the least, I thank each and every dentist who took the time to respond to the letter of solicitation I wrote, asking for humorous stories. My sense of gratitude to these colleagues is all the more profound, when I consider *they didn't know me from Adam.* Hopefully, the presentation of their humorous anecdotes and wacky characters, will serve to put a smile on the face of each and every person who reads volume I of GRINNING & GRINDING...to the best of my knowledge, a first of its kind.

INTRODUCTION

*A*t this period of time in our nation's history, there are presently a number of best selling books describing the unraveling of the social, economic, political, and family fabric I simply took for granted as a boy back in the '40s and '50s. So many of us are in this age group, and, even though we recognize the truth for what it is, these books are somewhat frightening. They are presentations which, unfortunately, are able to document the tangible decline in a great invention which has allowed so many Americans to live life on a higher level than most anywhere else in the world.

Now we find ourselves wondering what will be the standard of life for our children, as we read these anxiety laden accounts. NO, these books are not based on fantasy or subjective speculation, nor have they been written by high-browed erudites, out of touch with reality and the common man. One of these momentous authors, George Will, is a man who is intellectually balanced and in touch with the pulse beat of American society. How else could it be, considering his appreciation and scholarly affair with baseball.

The heaviness of so much of the literary landscape I'm viewing at the moment, coupled with an irritation I receive when I hear individuals moaning and groaning about *their* job related stress, somehow stirred enough motivation to make a personal attempt at lightening things up a bit. Look, I'm 52 years old! You know I understand whistling in the dark won't make the boogey man go away. I knew it as a kid, but I learned, just like many of you, it could change those awful night sounds into something more tolerable. After a while, the whistling would start to be fun, and I'd begin to completely focus on the tune. I'd forget about the demons lurking out there.

I grant, certainly at first blush, this is sort of a screwy union for siring an offspring of humor. However, let me first tell you why listening to individuals griping about their job-related stress, with silence most of the time, has always made me want to scream from the tips of my toes, "You need to hear about some *real* job-related stress!" This book is my controlled scream to those individuals. But, after doing that, I have to admit there's really little else to say about the "unraveling books'" siring influence, except they were definitely part of the birthing of **Grinning and Grinding**, a book which has come at the precise moment when it seems most needed...

Have you observed the attire of dental professionals lately? If not, take a long, hard gander the next time you visit the dental office. Today, in many of the offices, you can actually find dentists and their staff dressed like latter day Apollo astronauts...their get-up more appropriate for a moon landing, than performing the fine finger movements so essential in dentistry. Now, that's just for starters!

Since the sweeping hysteria of AIDS and OSHA guidelines hit the dental scene, these health care providers have become donned and draped in goggles, gloves, gowns, masks and, sometimes, actually seen wearing god-awful galoshes-like bags over their shoes. It's a miracle no broken necks have been reported, caused by these natural death traps being worn on the feet of some of the more compliant ones.

You won't hear about me having that experience! Anyway, these professionals now work in offices that smell more like a toilet just swabbed with pine sol, or some similar rank-smelling disinfectant, than the old eugenol smell of my youth. Hell, I actually go around dropping eucalyptus oil throughout the office, just to make it *smell right.* Sometimes, I even burn incense.

Then, there is the new recommendation for posting of biohazard warning labels. Again, if the dentist is cooperative and compliant with government guidelines, he or she will have these warning labels posted throughout the office premises, particularly in the operatory and laboratory areas. I'm telling you, there are so many of these biohazard labels in my office, it looks more like a nuclear reactor facility than where I'm doing my dentistry, my grinning and grinding. I mean, really, the dental office isn't a potential **CHERNOBYL,** but one certainty would not know it by the warnings **OSHA** has advised dentists to paste on their equipment and supplies. I am looking for them to come up with a warning label for our handpieces, maybe even our very hands...any day now.

So, if fogging goggles, blood-constricting gloves, oxygen-depriving masks, confining gowns, or garbage bag-like shoe covers are not enough for these poor devils to deserve some humorous relief, what about the economic stress suffered by many of the nation's dentists? Big surprise, huh? I don't know why it should be...consider the fact they are multiplying out of dental schools faster than cockroaches on a midnight run for food crumbs. Then, consider the potential adverse affect OSHA might be causing...how hard do you think it is to sell a patient on a full mouth set of x-rays when they see a radiation warning label posted right in their face, while the dentist is doing his or her dead-level best to convince them routine dental x-rays pose little to no potential harm. Would not most patients, even those with one eye and half sense, consider this was nothing more than pure sales bull? Particularly, when they are staring at the warning for a potential "radiation melt down" right in their kisser. Hope you get the picture.

Oh, and please consider the now nebulous Clintonian creation...health care reform. Okay, so it's on the back burner, for now, but we health care providers know it's still out there, somewhere in the future's murky mist, just waiting to suddenly spring upon some of this country's **most beloved and popular professionals...**

Yes, that's right. My colleagues and I are insecure about being loved by our patients. Let me tell you what it stems from... "Doc, I don't dislike you, not personally, but I DETEST what you do for a living." Or, how about: "I DESPISE being here! I'd rather take a beating or a dose of poison, than sit through this. Most Of all, I HATE that damn drill of yours!" Now, accepting that's what we used to hear a lot of in the old days, actually not so long ago, and even though much of the fear and anxiety is a vestigial remain of the past, it is still heard enough to create a sense of leprosy-like loathing by those who receive our services. Actually, today, the fear of physical pain has been replaced with a generalized patient **fear of financial rape.**

Hopefully, you are beginning to see dentistry from a different perspective. It is loaded to the gills with stress, more today than at any point in its history. Certainly more than I can remember during my 25 years of performing dentistry. Is it any wonder I chose to create a book affording humorous relief to the poor creatures who practice it, and, of course, for those tortured souls who must enter and subject themselves, periodically, to the pains and perils of an office visit to...PURGATORY!

In response to an inner urge to inform you about how I gathered the material for writing this book and how I put it together, let me explain the technical mechanics. First, I sent a letter to hundreds of dentists asking them to submit one or more humorous experiences which had happened to them during the course of their dental education or practice career. Every story had to be true! This was the only rigid requirement I made in my letter of solicitation. Their cooperation was widespread and wonderful.

Secondly, after writing about some of my own experiences, I creatively edited the reports I began to receive from around the country. Sometimes my imagination, like any good Southern story teller worth his salt, turned **wild and woolly**—I readily admit that. But, always, I never strayed far from the central core of truth contained in each of the accounts sent to me. I might have used some expletives, for stronger adjectives, and you have my mea culpa (sorrow for my sin) if that offends you. I did it for their incomparable impact of the moment, and because they are the words of life the way so many Americans have come to see, hear, and actually live it, day to day, in the 1990s.

With that being said, why don't you now remove your shoes (if your feet do not first require fumigation with Dr. Scholl's), kick back, get comfortable, and start reading about some of the crazy things that have happened in a place where you might least expect it...the dental office. A place where fear and anxiety, even today, is never far removed from the potential of some sudden explosion, with comedic-like fallout.

Each story is like a bubble of time...wherein the patient's energy to contain their fear, and the dentist's expenditure of energy to control and direct that anxiety...is oftentimes burst by an unplanned upheaval at the scene. Then, and only then, does some release-like valve open, turning loose this pent up energy in the form of a light-hearted chuckle or, at times, fall-down-on-the-floor, side-splitting laughter. Hopefully, you may experience the full range of this phenomenon in many of the short stories found in this book...at least, you'll hold the demons at bay while whistling for a while.

—J. J. Portera
November 20, 1994
Jackson, MS.

GRINNING & GRINDING:

A COLLECTION OF AMERICA'S DENTAL HUMOR

"THE SCREW TURNS...."

*E*d, a good friend and patient of Dr. Fred Weyh, was an avid hunter, fisherman and art teacher for the local high school. He was, however, perhaps better known for being an inveterate prankster. He was always playing pranks on his friends. To all who knew him, Ed was said to be a man who lived life to its fullest. A man whose love for fun and people was so great, it left no room in his life for fear....except when it came to dentistry.

The thought of visiting his friend Fred Weyh, professionally, literally paralyzed him with fear for years. Fear, so profound that when he finally reported in for a long overdue checkup, he had developed an advanced case of periodontal disease (a condition whereby the gums are enlarged, bleed, fill with infection and in its final stages, causes enough bone destruction for the teeth to become loose; at this point, it's difficult for the patient to eat).

Ed's case was so advanced, it was hopelessly untreatable. Elimination of the generalized infection

1

would require removal of all his remaining teeth and the construction of an "immediate denture" (a set of false teeth which are made prior to the patient's own teeth being removed and, on the day of extractions, inserted immediately upon removal of the last tooth).

Fred Weyh, like a good friend, informed his old buddy "he'd take good care of him," promising not to hurt this man whose hands were cold, clammy and trembling as they discussed the removal of his teeth. Dr. Fred further advised Ed, even though he had been the butt-end of a number of Ed's pranks, he'd even make him **two sets of teeth**...one for the first few months, while shrinkage took place, and a second one about six months later. He assured Ed they would look "ten times better than those things in your mouth right now." Ed, with a cracking voice, agreed to make an appointment to start the procedure.

On the day the teeth were removed, Ed did unbelievably well. He could hardly wait for the placement of his "new teeth," as he heard Fred taking them out of the plastic sealed pouches lying on the counter top behind his head, then say....

"Well, Ed, how do you like these beauties.....?" Fred

asked, as he inserted the upper and lower dentures and immediately handed him the patient mirror....

The teeth Ed saw reflected were fangs a timber wolf, even Count Dracula, would have been proud to own. The cuspids (eye teeth) were protruded outward, rotated, and hung well below the patient's lower lip border. The front teeth, like old caricatures of Japanese kamikaze pilots, were wide and long, like large chicklets. They were horrible! Ed's response was short, but not sweet....

"You dirty Som-Va-Bitch!!!"

Aftermath: When Fred Weyh stopped laughing he gave Ed the real set of dentures. Ed, true to a nature which could not be changed, not even with a set of "Draculas," made a point of wearing his "Doc Weyh's teeth" to school once a year, to show everyone what a terrible dentist Fred Weyh was.....

—Submitted by: Fred Weyh, D.D.S.
Kearny. AZ

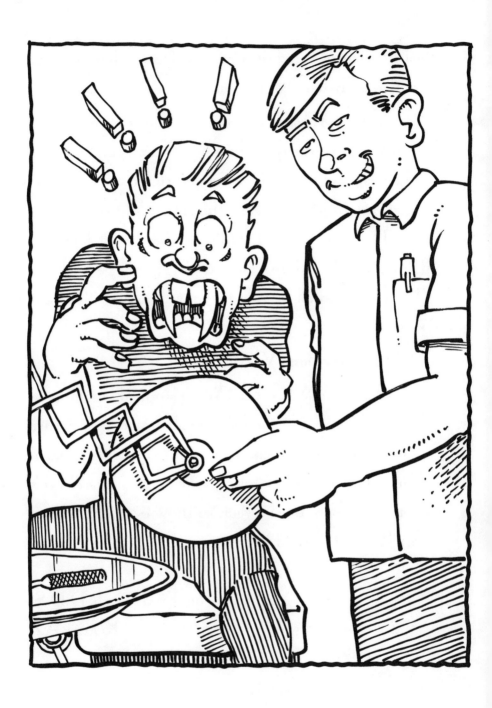

"ESTABLISHING PATIENT RAPPORT"

All professionals realize and concede the importance of establishing good rapport with a new patient or client on the first visit. That initial meeting in the dental, medical or legal office is usually the yard stick used to measure the office and personnel.

The following is an example of how to develop a fool proof practice builder....

One day, an emergency patient arrived at the office of Dr. Marc Chalkin. The man was obviously middle-aged, but looked somewhat younger, probably due to the jet blackness of his hair and mustache. Chalkin's assistant seated him in the dental chair and the dentist then proceeded to take the patient's medical and dental history. After listening to his chief complaint and completing the history taking, Dr. Chalkin advised the man he would need an x-ray to confirm the cause of his dental problem. He then walked out of the room in order that his assistant could take the radiograph.

Upon reentering the treatment room, Dr. Chalkin's eyes were immediately drawn to something lying on the floor, right beside the patient chair. His visual reaction was one of surprise, as confirmed by the question put to his assistant:

"My God, what kind of animal is that?" he said, bewildered by the thing on the floor.

His assistant, with a smile she was straining to keep from turning into laughter, pointed to the patient's head....now completely bald! The thing on the floor was his toupée! The x-ray head had apparently knocked it off while she was adjusting it for the shot.

With Dr. Chalkin's remark, the patient turned his attention to the ***"animal on the floor."*** His face immediately turned blood red! It might have been okay if the scene had stopped there, but, as these sort of things sometimes progress, it went from bad to worse.

"Would you please place that back on my head?" the patient asked the assistant. His tone was a mix of embarrassment, frustrated supplication, and subdued anger.

"Are you kidding? I'm not touching that....that

thing!!!!"

At that point, for some reason, Dr. Chalkin and his assistant burst out laughing. They couldn't seem to stop. It was like Poe's *"imp of perverseness"* had taken hold of them and both were seeing how fast they could destroy the potential for this man becoming a new patient.

Yes....that's right....they never saw the patient again! Their reaction to his hairpiece falling off is apparently not one to put in the practice-building lexicons of dentistry.

—*Submitted by:* Marc S. Chalkin, D.M.D.
Toms River, NJ

"IT SHO HAD A BITE....!"

This, the story of "John L.," confirms when a man is "in his cups," the level of his sensory perception diminishes in direct proportion to that amount which he has recently consumed....or, the sum total of all his consumption in the past. In the case of John L., it was a bit of both.

Drs. Hageman and Pippen, both with first names of Robert, were at the V.A. hospital in Dayton, Ohio, during the early '70s. Dr. Pippen was the staff oral surgeon, and Dr. Hageman was doing a rotating internship, when they made the acquaintance of the inimitable John L.

According to Hageman, where he and Dr. Pippen are now in private practice in Casper, Wyoming, John L. reported in for treatment of a fractured mandible (broken lower jaw). From their information, it appeared reasonable to deduce that John L. had suffered the injury while partaking of his favorite liquid nourishment....at one of his favorite "watering holes."

John L. may have been inclined to get into fisticuffs,

ipso facto (by the very fact), that he had the same first name as one of this country's great bare knuckled heavyweight boxers, John L. Sullivan. Maybe he was always being challenged by some other drunk, one who perhaps had the nickname of some other erstwhile champion. Who knows? A drunk's behavior, trying to explain or justify it, is strictly speculation and futility, at best. Most likely, his inclination to drink, then fight, was due to a deficit gene somewhere in there.

Non obstante (notwithstanding) my attempts at amateur psychological profiling of this character, Dr. Hageman's and Dr. Pippen's treatment of his broken jaw required six weeks of intermaxillary fixation (an oral surgical procedure which wires the upper and lower teeth together....an excellent way for losing weight, if one is so inclined to take such drastic measures for denial of food to one's stomach).

Before going on, it should also be noted that the character holding the lead role in the cast of our dramatis personae had another trait worth mentioning....possession of a gregarious nature, especially talkative when drinking. One afternoon, after having spent the better part of the day partaking of the "hair of the dog," John L. decided to stop by the oral surgery clinic and visit with his doctor friends. He was *seriously* inebriated....

Dr. Hageman had just finished removing two impacted third molars on a young veteran (wisdom teeth which were imbedded in the bone and unable to erupt). A matronly assistant of Drs. Hageman and Pippin, as was her usual custom, rinsed the two wisdom teeth off, both intact and unbroken from the extraction procedure, and placed them in a plastic cup containing a mixture of water and pure alcohol....she would dispose of the teeth some time later! Anyway, she placed the cup on a shelf above the sink, next to the clinic door entrance....

As John L. entered the oral surgery suite and began to exchange his slurred pleasantries with Dr. Pippen, the assistant and Dr. Hageman, he noticed the cup on the shelf. Apparently, the prior alcohol he had consumed all morning did not fill the octane rating requirement, or quantity, for John L., and before anyone could stop him, he picked the cup and downed the contents. But, somehow, he didn't get all the contents down....

He bent over, spitting out the two recently removed upper third molars into the sink. *None of the liquid came out with the teeth!* In amazement to the doctors and assistant, he continued with his conversation without blinking an eye or saying a word about the teeth he had just spit out in the sink.

After finishing whatever he was talking about, John L., in his usual abrupt fashion, turned to leave the clinic. Even though Pippen, Hageman, and the assistant were bug-eyed and opened mouthed, Dr. Hageman did manage to get the following out before John. L. was out the door:

"John L., what'd you think about those molars you just spit out?"

"Oh, hell, Doc, that ain't nothin a 'tal. I've had some likker so stout it'd uprooted least one mo toof. It sho had a bite tho....I's got to mit that....!"

—*Submitted by:* Robert A. Hageman, D.D.S.
Casper, WY

"THE LEAKING BRIDGE..."

A registered hygienist, by formal training, is that part of the dental team whose primary task is to clean the patient's teeth and educate them on the home-care techniques essential for maintaining dental and soft tissue health. A secondary role of the hygienist, sometimes spoken but not always, is the expectation and hope, by the dentist, that she *will sell dentistry.* Selling, in this instance, meaning she will reinforce and recommend that missing teeth be replaced with fixed or removable bridges, crowns for teeth that have large and leaking restorations or some other less than ideal status, cosmetic improvements with whatever restorations or procedure is most appropriate and other treatments the dentist may or may not have recommended at prior appointments.

Dentists are often told, at practice management seminars, to hire a second or third hygienist, instead of taking on an associate...another dentist! If the ad-

vice is not 100 percent accurate, it is, nevertheless, quite sound. Sound because that secondary role of the hygienist, when really put into practice, makes the office money....the bottom line for any business, be it healthcare delivery or selling ships. Some hygienists, naturally, are better at "selling" than others. There are those who do it with words and those who can do it with a *form of silence*....like the hygienist in the office of one Texas dentist.

A 35-year-old male was in the office for his six-month recall visit (teeth to be scaled and polished, bitewing x-rays taken to detect decay between the teeth, and home-care instructions). Essentially it is a routine check-up as done in most conscientious dental offices. The hygienist, Cindy, had completed the cleaning and was in the process of checking each tooth and restoration when she discovered a fixed bridge was loose on one of the two teeth it was attached to....

"Oh, my goodness, Mr. Johnson, it looks like your bridge is loose, and leaking...." Cindy said, as she probed around the margins of the patient's crowns with her explorer. Before continuing with her spiel on the need for removal of the bridge and possible remake, two things happened. First, she accidentally emitted some quite strong hydrogen sulfide gas (polite parlance)....she farted (in crude but common terms). Secondly, the patient quite rudely interrupted her with....

"Yeah, I know, I've heard Dr. Gerrard tell me that before....I know, I'm going to have to have a root canal, or something like that, if I don't go ahead and do something about it now," Roy Johnson interrupted, with clear comprehension of his problem and, just as clearly, his nonverbalized desire to put off the financial outlay for a new bridge. He had just completed his non-cooperative response *when he smelled it....*

"Whoa....my God, what's that horrible smell?"

"It's your leaking bridge, Mr. Johnson!!!! You've obviously been accumulating a few meals underneath the loose crowns. Has Mrs. Johnson said anything about your....?" The hygienist quickly fired back, knowing her deadly eructation had been silent. And, knowing the patient would never, not in a lifetime, think a beautiful hygienist would ever pass gas in a patient's presence, not even silently!

"If that odor's coming from my mouth, you get Dr. Gerrald in here, right now! I'm ready to do that new

bridge. I can't believe he hasn't told me I needed to get...."

Dental Moral: A dedicated and loyal hygienist should be ready to break wind, silently, of course, if it is the only avenue open to making that "dental sell"....for essential work of course!

—*Submitted by:* Anonymous contributor
Houston, Texas

"THE ESCORT BUSINESS....."

*D*r. Ron McCollor, a retired dentist living in Sun City West, Arizona, loved the practice of dentistry, particularly the talking and joking around with his patients which private practice provided in abundance. One of Ron's most entertaining and memorable conversations took place with a patient named Lee. McCollor described him as "a little tiny guy, about 120 pounds, pale, drawn, about 65 years old." Ron, a pretty good-sized guy, all tanned from the Arizona sun, like most natives, found this guy's appearance stimulated his curiosity....

Ron: "Gee, Lee, you're not very tanned for being a native of Arizona...."

Lee: "Yeah, I know. A lot of people say that about me....but, I work at nights!"

Ron: "Oh, is that right?" McCollor responded, while glancing over at the patient's chart.

'Well, no wonder the guy's pale and emaciated....he's

working hard at nights,' Ron thought to himself as he read under **occupation,** the patient had listed **"escort service."**

Ron: "Hey, Lee, tell me something about this escort business! I've never met anybody in the escort service....let me in on that!"

Lee: "Well, I'll tell ya...what we do in the escort business is like if you have a big bulldozer, or an extra-wide house trailer, something like that, we block off the traffic at two or three in the morning so you can get it out of town."

Ron: "And, that's what you call that kind of business?"

Lee: "Yep."

Ron: "Well, I'll be darn. I didn't know that. I thought you just called it the moving business, or people movers, something like that...."

Lee: "Oh, no, it's the escort business," the patient said, with emphasis on **escort.**

Ron: "Well, are you actually listed in the yellow pages under **escort business?**"

Lee: "Yes, we are."

Ron: "You've got to get some interesting calls?"

Lee: "Oh, we get 'em all the time! I had one just the other day."

Ron: "Tell me about it," his curiosity now focused like a cat on a bird.

Lee: "A woman called up and asked me if this was the escort place. I said, "yes it is." She said she was looking for a man. *I explained the only thing we handled was oversized loads and heavy equipment.*"

Ron: "What'd she say to that, Lee?"

Lee: "**O wonderful!** That's exactly the kind of guy I'm looking for....!"

—*Submitted by:* Ronald S. McCollor, D.D.S.
Sun City West, AZ

"STARCHED AND READY...."

This story, while running the risk of condemnation for being sexually suggestive, is yet another true account of dental delirium being experienced while practicing dentistry....

At about 9 a.m. one Thursday morning, my receptionist informed me that my new patient, Mrs. F. Patrick Humboldt, had been seated in the main operatory and was awaiting our introduction. This lady was old money, like money old enough to have a cedar or moth-ball smell. The kind that doesn't succumb to weekend spending sprees, swindlers, sycophants or the peer pressures which causes money of lesser antiquity to soon play out.

This was true mega bucks! Some of her acquaintances had described her as having more money than God. Her social standing was obviously with those of similar standing. However, the latter was not measured by the economic barometer alone, but through the kinship of being true aristocratic, southern blue-blood. She was the real thing! Entre' into her society is never totally realized by the nouveau riche'.

Mrs. Humboldt, like people of similar economic and social standing, was accustomed to having her way. Most of the time, she would insure this before making her personal appearance. This was certainly the case this morning as I had already received a phone call from the referring dentist, a week earlier, and he had taken great pains to let me know exactly *who* would "soon be gracing my office with her presence." His referral was specifically to obtain a consultation on the feasibility of doing a complete cosmetic reconstruction....Needless to say, I was going to have my office, my staff and myself looking our very best and being most affable. I needed to make an indelible impression.......

Immediately upon learning that *Mrs. "Porsche,"* I mean Mrs. Humboldt, was in the chair, I went into my private bathroom to relieve myself, wash up a bit, comb my hair and straighten my tie. I wasn't Lord Chesterfield himself, but I definitely intended to make sure I looked like I knew *GQ* was a men's fashion magazine and not something to remove oil spots from overalls. I even splashed on some very appealing cologne. I felt irresistible....

As I neared the operatory, I gave my hair one last comb with my fingertips and walked in with an aura of confidence and amiability which I felt would guarantee the patient's acceptance of any recommendation I made, if, for no other reason, than my demeanor and looks alone....

It was precisely at the moment I extended my hand and made initial eye contact with her that I intuitively sensed something was amiss. The feeling took place somewhere deep inside that part of the brain which never fails to alert one to something not being just right. Yes, I knew something was wrong, but like people will often do when experiencing similar feelings, I believed if I could just get a conversation going, and keep it going, the feeling would simply go away.

I glanced quickly at my dental assistant for reassurance that everything was okay. I searched her eyes for any hint of assurance that my feeling was simply a moment of self-consciousness or perhaps insecurity....I received the same sensation I had when I made the eye contact with the patient! Now I knew something was definitely wrong in the old ballpark. But 'what?' I thought, as my brain raced for answers.

I saw growing grins on both of their faces, and thereby reasoned neither had concluded I was a child molester, masquerading as a dentist. Next, I deftly checked to see if something was hanging or dripping out of a nostril. Again, my brain registered a negative! 'What then?'

All the while I continued to conduct a most gracious and entertaining conversation with this lady....while my eyes and smiling face expertly belayed my brain's anxiety and trepidation that egg was somewhere on my face. 'But, where?' remained the question I kept asking myself.

Then, with lightning-like awareness and perception, my eyes caught both of *their subtle, but downward glances* toward my....yes, *toward my crotch*. With a most graceful and agile movement, magician-like, true poetry in physical motion, I checked myself out....

'Oh my God, I can't believe this!' my brain said silently, the only thing keeping it muted being the sudden sight of that thing so many men dread; that thing so many old men have a problem with....the unzipped fly! But, mine wasn't just an open fly. Absolutely not! *Mine had a full eight to nine inches of starched white shirt sticking out, pointed, actually in an upright, curved position. It's resemblance to a.....yes, though strangely twisted and stark white, was undeniable!* If I had intentionally tried, I could not have arranged the shirt in a more suggestive or perverted position. I cannot adequately describe my embarrassment!

"Well, ladies, now that I'm sure you've been impressed with my imagination and creative sculpturing skills," I said, while deftly closing my zipper, **"why don't we see what we might be able to do, dentally..."**

With that, the subtle grins on their faces just seconds earlier, immediately grew into spreading smiles and chuckling. Then, this bubble of time, where tension had been tightly confined, suddenly broke and unleashed its energy in a volcanic-like eruption of open-mouth laughter as all three of us started howling....even the quite prim and proper Mrs. F. Patrick Humboldt.

Aftermath: I did do the case, and I used *my wonderful imagination and creativity* to cosmetically reconstruct Mrs. Humboldt's teeth with such realistic size, shade and anatomical form, that her *satisfaction* has brought me many, many referrals over the years....believe it or not!

—*Submitted by:* **The author**

"I GOTTA GET THE CREDIT....PLEASE!!"

*I*n dental education, a student is assigned a certain number of "units" or "experiences" to fulfill before he or she can receive a degree in dentistry. They were called "requirements," pure and simple, some 25 years ago. In essence, one had to perform a certain number of silver fillings, gold inlays, fixed and removable bridges, extractions and the other patient procedures which make up the full range of dental treatment.

These numbers take on life or death significance to a dental student. The only thing of relevance in their life, then, or now, no matter whether they are designated as experiences, guidelines or requirements, soon becomes the checking off of those procedures by a professor, to have the work duly credited to the student's academic account. Historically, a dental student will do anything, short of murder, to get credit for his work.

Robert J. was in his first year of clinic care....the time when a student starts treating his ***first live*** *patient*.....generally between the sophomore and junior year or in the first quarter of the third year. He was preparing to give his first mandibular block injection, in order to restore a lower left first bicuspid with a silver filling....

....The mandibular block, as explained in another story, is an injection dentists use to numb one half of the lower arch. When done correctly, it anesthetizes all the teeth from the last molar to the midline of the lower front teeth on that side of the lower jaw. Placement of the needle is critically important, since, if not guided into the tissues correctly, it can actually penetrate the facial tissues and emerge outside the cheek or area around the jaw. Obviously, this does not happen very often....

However, with Robert's first attempt on a live patient, the needle somehow got away from him and the tip of it passed through the cheek....spilling some of the anesthetic onto the skin of the cheek. He did not realize this, nor did the patient! Some two hours later, after a half dozen excuses and reasons for why the patient couldn't get numb, Robert dismissed her....with a very questionable silver filling having been done.

That night some six or seven hours later, the patient reached Robert by phone and indicated that she was in terrific pain. Pain so persistent and pernicious that she was going to an emergency clinic, *"to have this damn tooth pulled. I can't go through another session like we did today to try and save one little tooth."*

Humiliation and concern for the patient took a backseat to Robert's own sense of academic survival, as he responded to the patient's report and decision:

"Look, you do what you want to about getting the tooth pulled...just do me one favor, please! After you get the tooth pulled tonight, keep it, and bring it by the school clinic tomorrow. I gotta get credit for that silver filling....!!!"

—*Submitted by:* W. Jack Saxonhouse, D.M.D.
Boca Raton, FL

"WIVES IN PUBLIC RELATIONS...."

Somewhere in the book's introductory remarks, I distinctly remember failing to mention "worshiping wives," among other things, and this story is definitely about one of those lovely spouses. A dental wife, not unlike many I've known, has a major interest and concern for her husband's health....his financial or economic well-being! The prospering of his health being nourished by how much goodwill she, the dutiful and dedicated wife, can spread around with the patients and in the community.

Okay, not to be facetious nor to belittle our "better halves" in word or innuendo, let me say that all those unselfish efforts our wives are exerting on our behalf are deeply appreciated. It really doesn't matter what the motivations are, of course, we dentists simply say "thank you" to all our spouses at this time....

I also want to extend, at this point, a personal thank you to Adele Kunz, the wonderful wife of Dr. Ronald

A. Kunz. Her skills and finesse in practice building techniques for Ron's office are about to be presented....particularly, *her ability in creating patient confidence and trust in her words of praise!*

Adele, who is normally not in the office, "just happened" to stop by the office one afternoon "to see how things were going." She asked Ron's receptionist what type of work he was doing in the operatory and was told he was *"seeing a patient for new dentures."*

Now, the reader should see how intensely interested these dental wives are...Adele didn't ask for superfluous information, she went straight for the *dollar information*....I'm sorry, I mean directly to the type of labor Ol' Ron was doing back there at the chair. But, it is relative to point out a new set of dentures goes for between $450.00 to $2000.00, depending on where and who is doing the work. And it is an accepted fact in the dental community that denture patients are among some of the hardest patients to please, to put it mildly! They can be a royal pain in one's rear end!

As the patient, Mr. Smith, left the operatory and started to leave the office, Ron's wife just happened to meet him in the business office area, where she offered the following verbal observation:

"Oh, hello, I'm Dr. Kunz's wife, Adele," Ron's wife said, as she extended her hand to the patient. **"I have to tell you those dentures are really handsome looking! I know you must be very plea..."**

Before she could finish the praise spiel of her public relations efforts, the patient abruptly interrupted her with. **"Lady, these are not new dentures! These are my old dentures, thank God, because they sure as hell look better than those chicklets he's been fooling around with for the last three weeks,"** Smith said, with an irritated tone which indicated as we say in the South, "he hadn't come in on the turnip wagon, yesterday!"

Postscript: So, how's that for salesmanship and public relations? Let me rephrase....how's that for a dental wife praising her husband's dental skills? Is this not a beautiful example of having all the facts together before opening one's mouth, not to make a pun, or fun, of Adele Kunz's *"practice building work"*?

Sorry, Adele, the devil made me do it....After Ron gave me the basic picture.

—*Submitted by:* Ron A. Kunz, D.M.D.
Pittsburgh, PA

"Can I speak to Dr. Oxford.....?"

This is a story about two brothers, Al and Louis Oxford, who practiced together for over 30 years in Bristol, Tennessee.....

One afternoon, after the staff had vacated the office premises, Al and "Louie" were the only ones left in the office. The phone started ringing and Louis Oxford, being closest to the front office at the moment, found himself taking the following phone call....

Louie: "Hello, Dr. Oxford's office."

Caller: "Can I speak to Dr. Oxford?"

Louie: "Which Dr. Oxford do you wish to speak to, Al or Louis?"

Caller: "I can't remember his name, but this Dr. Oxford was very tall!"

Louie: "We're both about the same height. Do you want the one with brown hair or black hair?"

Caller: "I can't remember his hair color!"

Louis: "Can you remember if it was the one with the blue eyes or brown eyes?"

Caller "No, I can't!"

Louie: "Did you notice the name over the pocket on the white lab coat?"

Caller: "I didn't notice a name on the lab coat!"

Louie: "Well, let me ask you this....was it the ugly

one or the good-looking one?"

Caller: "*That* I do remember! It definitely had to be the ugly one."

Louie: "Great! I'll get my brother to the phone for you!"

—*Submitted by*: A. Bryant Oxford, D.D.S.
(son of Al Oxford)
Sedona, AZ

"LITTLE OLD LADIES DON'T LIE..."

*D*r. John Safarik was in that fateful week of his life when he was about to leave 39, the number Jack Benny stopped counting at, and turn 40. He had been bemoaning the upcoming event all week long. On one particular day during that dark week he happened to have one of the sweetest, little ladies he'd had in the chair in months. He recalls "she was a carbon copy of Whistler's mother...." probably in her mid 80's, wearing the standard little shawl over her shoulders, her bluish-white hair held in place by the little hair net and, of course, the ever-present knitting needles. He could not have conjured up or created a patient who would have been a better image of the proverbial "sweet, little old lady."

John recalls that his preparation to leave his 30's was anything but graceful. He had been raving and ranting, on and on, about the birthday coming up that weekend. He continued to talk about how old he was getting, mentioning how he could tell his racquet ball

game was slowing, as well as his thinning hair and the fine wrinkles which were beginning to show, more and more, around the corners of his eyes. He hated the thought of turning 40, and all his patients and staff people were hearing about it, non-stop!

Then, in a moment of self-awareness of how depressing all his moaning and groaning must be sounding to his patients and staff, particularly to a person who was now in her eighth decade, he immediately decided to try and sound more upbeat, more optimistic....

"However, you know how the old saying goes, 'life does begin at 40!'" Dr. Safarik said, directing his words and eyes toward the little old lady in his chair.

His sweet, little old lady instantly dropped her knitting needles into her lap, looked over the top of her Ben Franklin glasses, and said, **"Dr. Safarik,....that's pure Bull Shit!!**

—*Submitted by:* John J. Safarik, D.D.S.
Carlsbad, CA

"THE GREAT COMMUNICATOR...."

All of us, to some degree, have an appreciation for the importance of good, clear communication between a patient and his doctor. This story...submitted by a dentist who not only saw himself as a pretty good patient communicator, but had the notion generally reinforced by many of his colleagues...reveals how a self-portrait can oftentimes be a picture whose image is perilously out of focus to the patient.

Another point which comes across to me, after the full enjoyment and digestion of the obvious humor, is the "over-talking" many professionals are guilty of with their patients. If it's not *technical* talk which is over their head, then it is frequently *over* talk in terms of mere volume.

Lawrence Schiffman had been out of dental school about five years and thought he was "a second Abraham Lincoln," when it came to communication skills. He felt particularly gifted in being able to clearly explain the patient's overall dental needs, or when it became necessary to refer them to a specialist. By his own measurement, Dr. Schiffman felt he was going along very nicely, until he met the patient who caused him to do some serious soul-searching.

It seems this patient, a middle-aged, "tough as nails" woman, satisfied the criteria for having moderate to advanced bone loss and was therefore referred to a periodontist (a gum specialist). Dr. Schiffman spent considerable time advising the patient on what she might expect and encouraged her to call him if she felt the periodontal specialist was not adequately answering any questions she might have....

The first clue that some serious communication gap had taken place was with the patient's remark to him on a subsequent appointment....

"Well, how'd your first visit with the periodontist go?" Larry asked, as he prepared to do some minor operative work (fillings) which the periodontist had recommended he go ahead and do.

"Okay, I guess. But, I can tell you, I don't appreciate being charged $600.00 for tooth brushing instructions. Not a damn bit, Doctor!"

With that reaction, Dr. Schiffman now admits he should have stopped right there and gone to the bottom of why the patient thought she was paying $600.00 for instructions on how to brush her teeth. But no, Larry dove in head-first. He went on and on, about why it was so essential to have her home-care maintenance tightly nailed down before starting with the gum surgery. Oh, hell, he even branched out into a discussion of specific osseous (bone) and various other soft tissue surgical procedures which were anticipated in her case. In a word, he got very, very technical in the hopes that this might explain the $600.00 fee for *"tooth brushing instructions."*

Two weeks later, the woman showed up at his office, unexpectedly, and indignantly accused him and the periodontist of everything but being gentlemen. Since Larry might be a little reluctant to actually divulge what was said, let my *imagination* assist him, particularly since he might have experienced some memory loss due to the trauma of the encounter....

"Dr. Schiffman, let me tell you what I think of you and that gum gardener. I think you are both *crooks*, in cahoots to rob and steal from patients you assume are

as ignorant as rocks. I want you to know I think you are both as low as whale excrement! Okay, have I made myself perfectly clear to you?"

Larry Schiffman tried to calm the *creature* down, but unfortunately, every time he tried to say something, she would call him "liar." The tirade started afresh when he tried to tell her his only desire was to get her gum disease cleared up....

"What a helluva liar!" she rudely interrupted. **"Let me get the rest of this off my chest, you *thieving mongrel.*"** At this point, Larry Schiffman figured she would have a mat of thick black, curly hair all over her chest, if he just had the nerve to reach out, grab her blouse and yank it open. Apparently, discretion was the better part of valor, because I have not been apprised if she actually had that much hair on her chest, or not.

She continued: **"First, you and that *cheat* conspired to charge me 600 bucks to teach me how to brush, like I'm some kind of five year old kid. Then, that S.O.B. of a gum gardener sends me a bill for a procedure he had already stated would be done *free!* I've got a good damn mind to sue you both for malpractice....!"**

Lawrence gave her time to vent all the steam. This

44

time waiting until it was all out before he tried to reason with her. Fortunately, he was learning quickly, because this time she was quiet enough to hear him out. Of course, it may simply have been a case of vocal exhaustion.

"Mrs. Stockton, I really would like to know what procedure the periodontist charged you for, which was to be "free" according to the initial plan of treatment he had presented to you."

"I certainly will tell you, and I hope you check this out before you send another patient to that *fleecing scoundrel*. Yes, that son-of-a-gun charged me for a procedure that was listed on the statement of services rendered as **"free gingival graft."** Now, what do you think about them apples, Doctor?"

....the "free gingival graft" is a procedure done by periodontists and so named because of how the graft is obtained in the mouth. In essence, it is named due to the manner in which the tissue graft is obtained for transplanting to another location in the mouth....*it had absolutely nothing to do with a typo error on the patient's bill. Just another example of obscure communication*, the type that does not make for an accurate patient interpretation of what is being done....

Postscript: "Just the other day," Dr. Schiffman told me, "I discovered experience is, indeed, the best teacher. Another patient of mine returned from the office of the same periodontist and described the 'tissue graft' she received....the word 'free' had never been uttered nor was it even listed in the code of procedures offered by this periodontist"....believe it or not!

—*Submitted by:* Lawrence Schiffman, D.M.D.
Hudson, OH

"SUTTON'S DISEASE"

*W*hile Dr. Hageman was in his oral surgery residency, there was a junior resident in the program whose last name was Sutton. During one of the rotations, it was the surgery resident's duty to spend some time in the dental school's oral surgery clinic. This was done, supposedly, to afford the dental students some of the resident's expertise in taking out impacted third molars (a resident, in medicine or dentistry, is an individual who has already received his medical or dental degree, and is then in some specialty training program.)

One day while Dr. Sutton was on this rotation duty in the dental school, he had a young lady in the chair for removal of her two upper third molars. He proceeded with removing the first one and, just as he elevated it from the socket, she swallowed the tooth....the patient's extremely small mouth might have contributed to the accident.

Seeing no visible signs of distress or choking, and the other tooth already being numb, Dr. Sutton thought, no doubt, it would be better to go ahead and get it out before taking her downstairs to the radiology department, for x-rays to determine where the tooth was now located. After all, any of us might have made the same decision, figuring the odds were against anything else happening to the patient.....

Abyssus abyssum invocat (one miss-step leads to another. Lo, and behold, Sutton starts to elevate the second wisdom tooth out of the socket and, unbelievably, this one also goes down the patient's throat.

The patient was taken to the radiology department, and it was confirmed that both teeth were in the stomach, fortunate for her, and not somewhere in her lungs.

The next week, during the clinical pathology conference (a formal time the residents use for presentation of patient cases, some being rare and unusual ones, others not so out of the ordinary), a slide suddenly appeared on the screen, much to Dr. Sutton's chagrin, with the following oral description.... **"The following is a classic case of Sutton's disease...."**

There, on the screen in vivid color, was the x-ray of a patient's stomach containing two third molars!!!

—Submitted by: Robert A. Hageman, D.D.S.
Casper, WY

"It's a job for Flo...."

"*D*r. J." of Los Angeles, has a patient in his practice whom, for purposes of anonymity, we will refer to as "Mr. A." The patient wears a toupée which is not the most realistic hairpiece in existence. In point of fact, if one could purchase a man's hairpiece at a major discount center, it would be described as a K-Mart model rather than one found on Rodeo Drive or some other fashionable and expensive shopping area of the country.

In the words of Dr. J., before he learned how to work with Mr. A. and his hairpiece, the following event took place....

"Mr. A. was seated in the chair and I was doing a crown preparation on a lower right molar, his head cradled between my left arm and that side of my body. My assistant, as with most right handed dentists, was seated on the left side of the patient. As I worked, Mr. A's toupée would move a little, at which time he would push it back in place. My assistant would give me a little smile each time his hairpiece moved out of position. It looked, in a peculiar sort of way, like the top of his head was slipping off each time the thing moved a little.

After about five or six times of repositioning his toupée, Mr. A. reached up, obviously disgusted with the poor job his toupée's tape was doing, removed the hairpiece and, with a look of disgust, handed it to my assistant with the request that she put it away until the dental procedure was completed. The assistant, a young lady named Judy, was from Georgia. I'd never known her to be at a loss for words, but, this time, she was speechless. Finally, she put the hairpiece on top of the medicine cabinet, then abruptly left the room and sent in my other assistant."

Dr. J's other assistant, Flo, was middle aged and had a subdued sense of humor. It was dry, low key and *never* delivered with a smile. She walked into the operatory, not speaking to either patient or doctor, sat on the assisting stool and, with a poker face and matter-of-fact tone asked:

"Doctor, shall I apply this...?" Flo asked, as she lifted the patient's toupée from the cabinet top with one hand, and indicated to Dr. J. she was holding a small tube of *super glue* in her other hand, behind the patient's head.

Having somehow maintained his own composure until the procedure was completed and the patient gone, Dr. J. could hardly wait to ask his young assistant from Georgia why she left the operatory so suddenly. Her response, in a slow, southern drawl was....

"Oh, Dr. J., ah'm so, so sorry ah left ya, but if I'd a'stayed in the room one more minute, I would've peed in my pants! I was a'laughin so hard by the time I got out of the operatory, I barely did make it to the bathroom....By then, I surely did know it was a job for Flo! Thank Gawd I wasn't pregnant, cawse my bladder couldn't a'stood his a head a'fallin awf one more time...."

Dental Moral: If a patient is suspected of wearing a toupée, the chairside assistant should immediately locate a tube of *super glue* and have it close at hand, for a similar contingency. Assistants, keep in mind.... **"a dab will do."**

—*Submitted by:* "Dr. J."
Los Angeles, CA

"THE WELDER"

I was in my second year of private practice, about 28 or 29 years old, short on experience, but long on naiveté and had that enthusiastic desire to please, almost to an abnormal degree, that so many young dentists possess when starting their practices.

I had located in a fairly rural area, with many of my patients coming in from Arkansas and northwestern Mississippi. One of the patients was a middle-aged welder, originally from the Ozarks area of Arkansas. He, unfortunately, but like a considerable number of people from that area, had very little formal education and as a result (combined with years and years of hearing a certain type of rural dialect in the area), his english was not the king's, to make a tremendous understatement. This man's name was Bill, and he came in by way of referral from a relative of his whom I had made a full denture for a few months earlier. Bill was also to have a complete denture made. It was his first!

One afternoon, at the point when the denture teeth are still in wax in order that we can reposition them if necessary, the following episode took place.

I was starting to use a piece of dental equipment which is black, about 12-14 inches in height, and utilizes a wick that extends into a tank inside the instrument which is filled with denatured alcohol. It has a small finger trigger which, when pumped will project a jet of air over the lighted wick and thus give the dentist a very small, but quite intense flame. It is used to heat and soften the wax thereby making it easier to rearrange the teeth, if needed.

Anyway, as I started to use the "miniature torch," Ol' Bill suddenly leapt out of the chair and, with both hands extending out in front of him, in a push-me-off position, made the following excited protestation:

"Whoa boy! Jus you wait a dayum minit, now. I sho nuf hurd you wuz mity good at keepin folks false teef in, but I be diddly damn if you gonna weld them thar sombithces in my mouf!"

Needless to say, I was ruined for the afternoon. It took me 15 minutes to get off the floor in my lab, because I had laughed so hard, and then another 10 minutes to calm and assure the backwoods welder I had no intention of "using the torch on him."

—The Author
Jackson, MS

"REASSURING SANITY...."

I believe most dentists would agree it is important to convey steadiness of hand.... no morning-after alcoholic tremors or similar neurological disorders....to a patient. I think they would also agree it is essential to impart a sense of calmness and overall emotional stability to their patients. In essence, since dental patients are not usually under the influence of general anesthesia and are therefore fully awake and aware of every minute detail going on in and around their mouth, it is all the more important to *nurture the idea*, at least, that the dentist and his assistant are "normal"....with no seriously, undiagnosed mental aberrations.....

It was 11 p.m. and the dentist and his assistant were exhausted from close to 12 hours of general dentistry. The dentist, a guy whom I personally know, just could not turn the emergency call down due to his terrific sense of concern and compassion for patients in pain. He agreed to see the man, even though he was on the verge of physical collapse. His assistant, not in much better shape, said she was ready and willing to help....even at this late hour and in spite of the rest and sleep her body was aching to realize.

The patient arrived, and somehow they seated him in the chair and placed the paper bib cover on him without the chain's metal alligator clip biting the skin of his throat or neck. The dentist even administered the local anesthesia (the shot) without so much as a flinch being elicited from the patient. Everything, in spite of their exhaustion, seemed to be going great. The patient was, of course, unaware of their physical states. "Dr. Archer," we'll call him, had just started drilling into the decayed lower left molar when it happened....

Dental assistants usually sit considerably higher than the dentist on their stools, when assisting. His stool is about 6 to 10 inches lower than hers. This is to give the assistant an unobstructed view of what's going on in the mouth. This is very important when she's using the high speed evacuation system (high speed suction tube with tip) to remove saliva and other debris as it accumulates in the patient's mouth.

Perhaps it was because she was bone-tired. Maybe not. It might have been a simple slip or loss of grip which might have occurred after 10 hours of sleep. Who can say? No matter, it did happen....she dropped the high speed suction tip, from her position above Archer's head, and due to her elevation above him as well as her close proximity, **the plastic tip hit her dentist right between the eyes, just above the bridge of his nose...and then, like some blood sucking leech, it stuck**. The vacuum-like suction insuring its union to Dr. Archer's skin.

The **imp of perverseness**, not the devil and Archer's nature of being the perennial nut I know him to be, caused him to do it....**he looked up at her, *cross-eyed*, and they both lost it!** Giggles, at first, then a quick transition into uncontrollable laughter, which was soon followed by paroxysms of it. The patient, at first oblivious to the incident was brought to full consciousness with their laughter. He looked up, at her, first, then at his dentist who still had the suction tip sticking to his head. The patient's only comment was....

"When did they let you two out of the cage?"

—*Submitted by:* Anonymous
New Orleans, La.

"Gold is gold....!"

One afternoon, back in the early '70s, with a patient in each of my chairs and four in the waiting room, my receptionist brought me a note indicating an 80-year-old gentleman was on the phone insisting I see him, "to replace the damn fill-

ing I'd placed in his tooth, yesterday."

It was apparent he would not take "no" for an answer, and, being the young dentist I was at the time, I wanted to do everything in my power to please patients with my work. Moreover, I had already discovered, from earlier treatment sessions with him, this man was a cantankerous old cudmudgeon. I could visualize him storming into the office, demanding treatment, if we didn't go ahead and try to accommodate his present demand.

After a few minutes of discussion with my staff, I advised the receptionist to "get back on the phone and tell him to come on in, right now! When he arrives, don't give him time to sit and visit with the other patients. You get him into one of the operatories as soon as he steps through the front door. I'll keep one chair empty until he gets here."

About 20 minutes later, Mr. Martindale's chauffeur escorted him into the reception room, since the old man had been declared *legally blind*. In fact the lenses in his glasses were as thick as the bottom of an old type soft drink bottle. Just as I had instructed, the receptionist took his arm and led him to the operatory furthest from the ears of patients in the reception room.

General William Tecumseh Sherman is supposed to have said, while torching the South and Georgia in particular, "Don't give them rebels time to sit and take a s....!" Well I wasn't going to give this old geezer time to sit and rest his bones while he trashed my work to the other patients. Again, I could mentally see and hear him, if given 20 to 30 minutes to beat his jaws together, instilling negative confidence in the minds of two of the new patients waiting to see me....

He couldn't have been in the chair more than 30 seconds, literally, when I walked in and said, "Good afternoon, Mr. Martindale. How are you?" (A mistake, of course. My present day dental dictum is to use that question with great caution and prudence when dealing with an irate patient. But, keep in mind, I was still very young and very naive, at that time in my career.)

"I'm not worth a damn, Doc!" he replied, in an acerbic and aggressive tone. I asked him, in the most stupid manner and tone I could muster, naturally, what the problem was....

"You know damn good and well your lady up front

told you that the *overpriced* filling you put in yesterday came out this morning at the breakfast table."

At this point, I had concluded, due to his authoritative accusation, the filling I placed had no doubt fallen out. However, for some masochistic tendency inherently a part of my youth, I asked him what he was eating when it came out....

"Some soft scrambled eggs and a half piece of toast. Hell, Doc, it came out before I ever started eating. It was while I was sipping my coffee!"

By this time, I was ready to look in the mouth to see if all the filling was out, or if some had remained in order to tell my assistant what procedure to set up. I said, "Mr. Martindale, let me look in there and see what's going on." (This is dental lingo spoken when grasping the mouth mirror in hand and positioning it for studying the teeth....assuming the patient is taking this obvious cue to open their mouth and let you visually examine the teeth.)

Suddenly, and quite unexpectedly, Mr. Martindale defiantly held his hand up, motioning me to stop, as he said, "Wait just a minute, Doc, I've got the whole damn thing here in my pocket!"

Finally, with the unfolding of at least 15 to 20 creases of a handkerchief he pulled from his trouser pockets, he emerged with something between his thumb and forefinger and triumphantly said, "Doc, here it is! Here's your damn filling," the old goat said, as he clumsily attempted to pass it to me. When I got it into my palm, I knew something was obviously wrong, big time! He had handed me *a gold watch stem*....

"Mr. Martindale, I'm sorry, but this isn't your filling. This is a watch stem!" I was now almost prying his mouth open with my mirror, and he had no choice but to open and let me see what the heck had happened to make him believe the restoration I'd placed yesterday had come out. Well, guess what, the silver filling I'd placed in his upper left 1st bicuspid was still in the tooth. However, an old gold inlay, probably there for eons, was out of the 2nd bicuspid.

"Uh, Mr. Martindale," I said, while slowly removing the mirror from his mouth, "the filling I placed yesterday is still in there. You do, however, have a missing gold inlay from the tooth next to the one I restored. You must have somehow managed to get the inlay and the watch stem mixed up in your pocket?"

With him being blind as a bat, I figured that was exactly what happened, but I wasn't ready, not with my wildest imagination, for the responses that followed.

"What's that you say, Doc?" he shouted loud enough to be heard on the street outside.

"You don't have a gold inlay here, Mr. Martindale. This is a watch stem. I can't put this in your tooth. We'll have to put a temporary filling in until you find your inlay, or we can take an impression to make you a new inlay." My voice was now on his level of speaking and hearing as my hygienist peeked in to determine what all the shouting was about.

"Aw, hell, Doc, what's the price?" He had definitely heard me, and the tone of his question let me know he felt I had a gun on him and was about to ask for his wallet.

"A two-surface gold inlay is $125, Mr. Martindale." (Can you believe the fees at the time?)

With my telling him the fee, I got the following response. Are you ready? This is the honest truth..... **"Hell, Doc, cement that gold stem in the damn hole! The son-of-a-bitch is gold isn't it?** *Gold is gold!***"**

Nothing I could do, no amount of explaining the technical considerations would budge the old goat. He was determined I'd cement the watch stem, and worse yet, he'd convinced himself it'd make absolutely no difference!

Now, for the first time since treating the old fellow, I suspected senility was rapidly gaining on good sense. Medically, I didn't know how much was pathological deterioration of his brain and how much was plain old hard-headed obstinacy. For that matter, I didn't know how much a tight-fisted hold on his money might be entering into the picture.

Doing my best to keep from laughing in his face, I pretended to put the stem in the tooth while actually placing a white type of filling we were routinely using in those days. I reasoned it was better not to do the silver type I'd done the day before, even though he was almost blind and three quarters deaf, because I wasn't sure of the degree of his senility. It might have been the type that came and went, suddenly, and I didn't relish him recognizing what was really taking place in a moment of complete lucidity. I wanted to avoid him possibly verbally rocketing into orbit....

As he left the operatory on the arm of my assistant, heading straight for the reception room and his waiting chauffeur, I overheard his obstreperous voice as he stopped to recount his chair experience and wisdom, with one of the patients still waiting to see me...

"Lady, if Doc says you need a gold filling, you'd better check at home to see if you have any old watch stems. It's the same thing you know. *Gold is gold!* Don't you let that young rascal tell you he can't use it, because he just did it for me. You save your husband some money. You hear me, honey?"

I still have the old man's watch stem somewhere around here, and I must admit, he entertained me for the entire time I practiced in that city. Anytime I'd slip up and ask him, "Mr. Martindale, how's that watch stem filling doing?" His invariable reply would be....

"Doc, that tooth feels better now than when that first piece of gold was put in there after the war......(World War I, of course).

This event actually happened in my office some 20 years ago.....believe it or not!

—*Submitted by:* The author
Jackson, MS

"Specialty Training Admired....."

*H*arry L. Switzer, a Phoenix dentist who practices general and hospital dentistry, had a patient about a year ago who was always asking countless questions about his oral and general health. It probably wouldn't have bothered Harry to answer them once, maybe even twice, but this elderly gentleman would ask the questions over and over again, no matter how clearly they had been answered.

One day the man was in for one of his dental visits and, while Dr. Switzer was in the middle of treatment, the patient asked him a rather unrelated question.....

"Doc, I've got this here rash on my rear end and nothing I put on it seems to work. Have you got any remedies I could try?"

Harry, being as patient as he could, explained that he didn't have any treatment recommendations for the rash and proceeded with the dental work. After completing the procedure, he turned his back to the patient and started writing his treatment for the day in the patient's dental record. Before he had finished the record entry, he was interrupted with....

"Doc, what do you think about this?"

Harry Switzer turned around to find the elderly patient out of the chair, his pants and shorts dropped down around his ankles, with a rash-faced moon, fiery red and shining right in his face. He was speechless for a second, then gathering his composure explained:

"Mr. Beeson, you can't drop your pants in here. I'm not a medical doc...."

At the moment he was about to get 'doc...tor' out of his mouth, he noticed the door to the hospital dental suite was wide open and there in the doorway stood one of the staff surgeons. A young resident was standing beside him. Both were staring in obvious puzzlement....

"Damn, Switzer," the surgeon said, after seconds which seemed like hours to Harry, "I didn't know you guys got training in proctology....."

—*Submitted by:* Harry L. Switzer, D.D.S.
Phoenix, AZ

"WHERE'S THAT MUSIC COMING FROM...."

Most present day removable partial denture frameworks are made of some combination of cobalt, chromium and molybdenum. These metals are usually alloyed with cobalt making up the greater percent of composition, and molybdenum the least. Years ago, gold was used quite frequently. Cost, and some improved physical properties of the newer alloys, has now made the use of gold in partial denture frameworks a thing of the past, for the most part.

The component of the partial denture which usually holds the teeth is a processed resin or hard plastic-like material. The latter is generally some shade of pink, in order to try and match the patient's gingival tissue coloration. We, as dentists, generally concede that the pinkish material is inert or incapable of transmitting hot, cold or much of any other stimuli for that matter. The metal, however, may well be another story, as one air force physician learned from a dental colleague.

A middle-aged woman from eastern Europe reported to the base dental clinic with a consultation form in her hand. She had been referred by the medical wing's family practice group. The patient's chief complaint, as spelled out on the physician's referral form, was her perception that she had been receiving radio transmissions through her partial denture framework ever since it was made in East Berlin, some two or three years ago.

The dentist immediately called the referring physician, who had been assigned the patient to determine if he was serious. The physician replied that he felt the patient might be suffering from schizophrenia, but, like most good physicians, he did not want to rule anything out. The dentist thanked him and assured the good doctor he would check the dental work very carefully....realizing, at this point, **one U.S.A.F. physician *had just set himself* up for some very interesting findings!**

Using a cardboard template, and some panorex duplicating film (a type of x-ray which will show most of the skull and teeth), **he *created* an x-ray which demonstrated an antenna in the center of the patient's head.** The x-ray and consultation form were returned to the referring physician with the following message:

"Antenna located. Please refer this patient to neurosurgery department for removal...."

—*Submitted by:* William T. Neely, III, D.M.D.
Plattsburgh, N.Y.

"What an Oral Surgeon!"

*D*r. Andy Garrott....my former student, friend, part-time genius, devotee of old things, devoted family man, dedicated dentist....is, besides these, a *fulltime nut case.* I make this statement, not despairingly, but to his credit and to the good fortune of those who come in contact with him. He, like individuals with a similar make up, often attract patients of like inclination. Consider the time...

An elderly lady, actually in her early 60's, but looking like a worn out bag lady, came in requesting a wisdom tooth be removed. The poor soul had never been to a dentist! She was missing most of her teeth, with five snags remaining, and firm about wanting the third molar out.

"You say you've never been to a dentist in your life?" Andy asked, curious after seeing all the missing teeth, with no apparent residual root tips remaining in the tissue like dentists oftentimes see with patients who have simply let their teeth rot off at the gumline.

"Yes sir, that's true fo sho...never been to a toof doctor in all my born days. This here is my very first time!" the old patient answered with what Andy perceived as pride in her voice.

"Well, Lula, whose been taking your teeth out all these years?"

"*Who* in the world do you thanks been a'takin 'em out, Doctor?" she responded, with a slight grin moving across her weather wrinkled face.

"Gosh, I don't have the foggiest notion. Was it old Doctor Jones?"

"No sirree. Won't him fo sho!"

"*You?*" Andy asked, not able to mask his incredulity.

"Yep, I's took them teef out, toof by toof....whenevar they's started to pain me pass my bility to stand it...."

"Lula, how could you remove your own teeth?" Andy's disbelief growing by the second.

"With *my toof puller*...." she said while fumbling with the rolled up handkerchief in the large, flower-print cloth bag in her lap.... "Yes sirree, with this here toof puller," she continued, while proudly holding up the instrument for Andy.

"My God, Lula! Why *that's a....a bent five-penny nail!* You took your teeth out with this?"

"Sho did! All ceptin this wisdom toof. I's tried, but can't gits a grip on it, or somethin...."

Andy removed the tooth and immediately showed the old lady why the severe curved roots had prevented her from being able to fully elevate the tooth out with her crude "*elevator...*"

"Lula, all I can say is you're one helluva oral surgeon! If you had a license and some real surgical instruments, I might put you to work with me...."

—*Submitted by:* L.A. Garrott, D.M.D.
Batesville, MS

"A MATTER OF SPELLING"

An elderly gentleman was escorted into the office of Dr. Greg Johnson, seeking relief from a painful tooth. Since he was a new patient, Greg sat down beside the old man and began to personally go over his health history questionnaire with him. Dr. Johnson did this out of deference to the patient's age as well as to determine the reason the patient had indicated with "yes," he had AIDS.

When Greg, in a somewhat halting and cautious tone, asked the patient did he, in fact have AIDS, the old gentleman's words were staccato-like and **loudly** indignant:

"Yeah, I got 'em, but they sure as hell ain't working so good!!!"

—Submitted by: **Greg Johnson, D.D.S.**
Charleston, S.C.

"Dead-eye Dick"

The following story gives a fairly accurate description of dental schools in the "old days," as well as a classical case of hysterical humor. I'm presenting it, almost verbatim, with the words used by the Kentucky dentist who went to school with this "five-year non-dentist..."

"At the time I attended dental school, patient care was delivered in one large room. The area was simply called, "the clinic." Our school must have had over 100 chairs in its clinic, and the space between each student dentist and his patient was no more than five or six feet, just enough for walking room between the dental units. It was nothing like the modern-day facilities which oftentimes have separate clinics for each problem area of dentistry.

During this time in dental education, the '60s, students did not begin actual patient treatment in "the clinic" until their third year of training. There was some initial patient exposure in the summer between one's sophomore and junior year. Basically, I think it's still pretty much like that today. Once we hit the clinic in our junior year, the mornings were usually spent in the classroom or laboratory and afternoons would be devoted to actual patient treatment.

The grades one received from patient care during those last two years of school determined when and if you graduated. Receiving a dental degree after becoming a junior, or even a senior for that matter, was *never a guarantee*. There were countless horror stories, as you no doubt can imagine, circulating about the unfortunate students (we used to say, "they didn't have the hands") who had sometimes been in school for four years, then flunked out. Tragic, but true. Some had even spent five years, where they might have repeated the junior or senior year, then were asked to leave. The system did not allow for an indifferent attitude.....generation X individuals would have a hard time accepting or adjusting!

Anyway, a guy named Benny was one of those unfortunate students who had repeated his junior year, twice, and was a senior the year I entered my last year. What made this guy's story all the more sad, really, was the fact the he possessed one of the highest I.Q.'s in our school. This was confirmed by the exceptionally high grades he made in the medical school courses we had to take as dental students. Benny had another problem, a trait which might be called an "attitude" today....his tendency to **never** admit he was wrong. A trait which did not ingratiate him to a lot of individuals, particularly the professors who had his life in their hands.

One afternoon with a heavy rainstorm going on outside, I found myself working in the unit next to Benny. I had started a porcelain jacket crown preparation on my patient's upper left central incisor about 20 minutes earlier, when I suddenly felt something wet hit my left hand. I immediately wiped the water off and looked up at the ceiling, thinking the roof might have started leaking due to the heavy downpour. Keep in mind, the building had been built in the early 1900s, and even though it had no prior history of leaking since I had become a student, it was raining bullfrogs. I think my reaction was quite normal. Seeing no evidence of water dropping from the ceiling, I went back to work.

One of the traits of character, either innately a part of the individual who ultimately becomes a dentist, or developed to a higher degree while studying dentistry, is the ability to concentrate and focus on the task at hand; I simply returned to the business before me.

About five minutes later, I again felt something wet hit my hand. This time I sensed it came from my left and, that it had force behind it. I glanced in that direction, towards Benny and his patient, the moment I felt the moisture. What I saw and heard is presented here for posterity:"

"Mrs. Evan, you **have** to be numb. **I probably have the deadliest aim in this school when it comes to giving a mandibular block!**" I heard Benny telling his patient.

".....The mandibular block is an injection dentists use to numb one half of the lower jaw. If done correctly, it numbs all the teeth on one side, from the last molar to the midline of the lower front teeth. The lower lip usually develops a tingling sensation, as the anesthetic begins to work. When giving the shot, the needle is guided along the inside of the ascending ramus....the bone which forms the backside of the lower jaw and attaches it to the skull. Students are taught to always direct the needle to the outside of their thumbnail, as they use the thumb to locate certain anatomical land-marks which prevent the needle from going to the out-side of the bone....."

"You have to numb! Anyway, supply has just given me my **last** carpule. **I can't give you another injection."** Benny continued, as I observed in total disbelief.

"......Back in those days, at our school for sure, we had an *old maid in charge of dispensing each and every item we used on patients.* Any expendable item was under her control and she would make today's computer chip appear pale and anemic, certainly not on par with her ability to mentally keep up with precisely how many carpules of anesthetic Benny had used thus far. This is not to mention the exact item and quantity some 60 or more students might have already used that afternoon. She was a **brilliant battle-ax!** Benny knew his chances of speaking to President Lyndon B. Johnson on the phone were better than receiving any more anesthetic from *"Ruth's supply room...."*

"You may be *dead-eye dick*, but I am not numb! I am sorry, but I cannot stand you touching my tooth again." Mrs. Evans, now noticeably anxious and upset, replied to Benny's remark about his deadly aim.

"I was walking towards Benny and his patient, even as she was making her remark. I called him off the side to tell him...."

"Benny, I know why your patient isn't numb!"

"What do you mean, not numb? **She has to be numb!** I've given her three blocks. She's just so damn nervous the stuff won't work," Benny responded, in his usual manner of self-denial.

"No, Benny, **there's no way she can be numb!**"

"What the hell do you mean, 'no way she can be numb?'" he reacted, his face now growing red with rage.

"Damn, man, you've got my left hand numb, but the only thing you can have numb on her is her right cheek or neck. Look at her neck, you idiot!" I responded, now heating up myself, because of his arrogant refusal to be objective.

"With my last remark, Benny turned and saw, in a milli-millionth of a second, what my eyes had seen the instant those second drops hit my hand. This guy, 'the deadliest aim in the school,' had directed the needle to the *outside*, instead of the *inside* of his patient's right ascending ramus bone and, with about **an eighth of**

the needle's tip sticking out of her right cheek, had shot me twice with a little over 1cc of lidocaine local anesthetic. The syringe had squirted it onto my hand like a water gun. A small amount of moisture could also be seen on the skin just below the angle of her jaw.

Just about the time we were completing our little aside discussion, and all had become painfully clear to Benny, the patient motioned for him to come closer as she gently touched the lower right side of her jaw and said, **'Gosh, Benny, I think we're about ready. I guess you do have a pretty good aim after all. I don't ever remember feeling quite this numb...it feels like the skin on my neck is even going to sleep....'"**

—Submitted by: Anonymous contributor
Lexington, KY

"YEAH, AND, I GOT A BRIDGE FOR SALE...."

*D*rs. Hageman and Pippin, oral surgeons in Casper, Wyoming, have an office policy whereby the patients referred to them are asked to come in for an initial examination and consultation before the actual work is done.

It's a great policy, allowing them time to explain the procedure which will be done, after affects, anesthetic options, potential complications and, best of all, to hopefully develop a good rapport with the patient....before doing the surgery. The whole concept offers an opportunity to allay fear and anxiety, which normally builds up before any type of surgery, before the patient comes in for anesthesia.

One afternoon, Dr. Hageman had scheduled a young boy in for removal of some deciduous teeth (baby teeth). Before taking the teeth out, Dr. Hageman immediately went into his routine of **"parte, non dolet"** (don't worry, it doesn't hurt).

Hageman, not having the advantage of being able

to conduct his usual pre-op consultation, since the boy was brought in from out of town, was simply trying to assure the youngster the tooth extractions wouldn't hurt, when he said. "Billy, I promise, this will be easy, and it won't hurt at all."

William "Billy" Gerard **was young**, but certainly in his own mind, **not stupid**. He had heard too many tales about.... **"broken jaws, roots wrapped around jaw bones and having to be dug out, thus leaving the patient with a numb lip for the next five years"**.....His response, based on the horror stories he'd heard from adults, and his somewhat precocious nature, was, **"Yeah, Doc, you get paid to say that stuff! Tell you what, if you think I be-lieve that stuff, let me tell you about this bridge I got for sale...."**

—*Submitted by: **Robert A. Hageman, D.D.S.***
Casper, WY

"THE WAL-MART SPECIAL"

*G*racie Mae had come in for the appointment to have her completed upper partial denture delivered by Dr. Andy Garrott. She had eagerly looked forward to this day for weeks, since she had long denied herself the dental work so desperately needed. Finally, after months of saving her money, she was now about to have her upper front teeth instead of the gap and snags of teeth she had endured for a long time.

Andy, a sensitive and compassionate person, was about as eager to place these teeth as his patient was to receive them. He had put so much of himself into this partial, actually having done the wax set-up himself....a procedure most dentists delegate to the commercial laboratory. He was like a kid at Christmas when he walked into the operatory with the partial denture in his hands....

"Well, Gracie Mae, the big day is finally here! Are you as excited as I am?" Andy asked with a genuine smile and excitement in his voice.

"Oh, my gawd, Doctor....lawdie mercy, I's so excited I's about to die!"

With her response, Andy laughed and proceeded with opening the sealed pouch which contained the partial. "I think you're going to like these beauties, Gracie," he said as he placed the prosthesis in her mouth, then motioned for his dental assistant to pass the round hand mirror to his patient.

Dr. Garrott, like many dentists, had actually started out of the operatory as the assistant was placing the mirror in his patient's hand. Dentists oftentimes do this in order to give the patient a feeling of no pressure being placed on them, by the dentist, to like the teeth. He was positive this patient would be extremely grateful and voice her approval. However, before he had even stepped out of the operatory, he heard those words no dentist ever wants to hear....

"Lawd, Dr. Garrott, these things looks like *beaver teef.* They's way too big...."

Andy couldn't believe his ears. He turned, looked at the teeth in her mouth, and told her to smile. Giving him the best smile she could, Andy responded with, "Gosh, Gracie Mae, they look perfect to me. You really look great! Why do you think they're too big?"

With a puzzled look she moved her eyes towards the mirror in her lap, and said, "Cause I can see fo myself. They's way too big....just you look here, again, " she said, motioning with the mirror for Andy to take another look. He did, this time looking in the mirror with his patient....

Everything instantly became clear.... "Oh, Gracie Mae, *you're looking in the **magnifying side** of the mirror.* Here, look in this side," Andy said, as he flipped over the round, chrome mirror bought at Wal-Mart.

"Oh, yes indeedy....now that's some sho nuf beauties, Doctor...."

—*Submitted by:* L.A. Garrott, D.M.D.
Batesville, MS

"Dentist With A Thousand Names"

If Lon Chaney could be called "man with a thousand faces," during his acting career, then this dentist is slowly but surely rolling up names for a somewhat similar title in dentistry. It all started with his spilling of the acid....

In dentistry we have some special types of restorations, usually fillings for front teeth, which require a dilute solution of phosphoric acid to be applied to the tooth structure prior to actually placing the tooth-colored filling material. The acid accomplishes or produces an etched surface, similar to sanding with fine sandpaper, and this allows the material to better adhere to the tooth. It is applied, many times, with a special pre-packaged syringe.

One afternoon, while our *dentist with a thousand names* was still in dental school, he received his first of the growing number of names he has apparently accumulated. Historically, his beginning occurred while in the process of doing a front tooth filling on a very attractive patient in her early twenties. Somehow he managed to get his hands on a clogged acid etch syringe and, after applying repeated and exaggerated thumb pressure to the plunger, the clogged portion finally gave way....spilling phosphoric acid over the patient's face and cornea. His classmates, **compassionate people all**, duly dubbed or christened him with his first name.....**The Joker**....the Batman character who had acid spilled on his face.

His second dental school nickname was conferred while attempting to remove a crown with a sliding weight crown and bridge remover....an instrument which looks like a stainless steel screw driver, with the tip being serrated and bent at a right angle to the shank. A cylindrical stainless steel weight, which will slide up and down the shank, applies dislodging forces once the tip is inserted below the crown or bridge margins. Essentially, one places the tip where the crown adapts at the gum line and, then, with rapid and successive upward motions on the weight, the crown will, if done correctly, come off. It is potentially a dangerous instrument and the dentist has to become quite adept at protecting the patient's surrounding structures. If the tip slips, as it does quite frequently, before finally dislodging the crown, well....

Our young dentist, still being in school, was not greatly experienced in the use of it, not to mention his inherent weakness in the area of natural manual dexterity. When the instrument's tip slipped and lacerated the patient's lip, requiring eight stitches by a plastic surgeon, he was titled, **Dr. Hook!**

His third name came when he drilled a patient's cheek with the carbide steel bur in a high speed handpiece turning at over 100,000 rpm. This also necessitated suturing by one of the Oral Surgeons on staff. It also gained him the name, **The Oilman.**

All total, his names came to 20 by graduation. The one that stuck, possibly the most outstanding and descriptive to colleagues of his abilities, or lack of, was **Dr. Iatrogenic**....defined, in medical terminology, as a **condition caused by the doctor!**

Postscript: I understand, from a reliable source, that

"Dr. Iatrogenic" is actually enjoying a successful dental practice, with no malpractice claims against him, re- markably, somewhere in the state of......

—*Submitted by:* Clifton Giorgaklis, D.M.D.
Brookline, MA

"SORRY....WRONG DEGREE, MA'AM!"

ary, a new patient, went to the office of Dr. Fred J. Weyh with an emergency.... the front part of her upper removable bridge had broken off and, with it, her two front teeth. An emergency for anyone. **For a female patient, a true dental disaster!**

Dr. Weyh informed the patient he could repair her removable partial denture, make her a new one similar to the one she was used to wearing, or make her the type which he considered superior in many aspects....a fixed bridge.

After informing the patient of what her options were, he then explained the details of appointment time needed for each procedure, as well as the difference in cost. He also covered, not being in a semi-comatose state or oblivious to the litigious nature of the society in which he lived and practiced his profession, the advantages and disadvantages of each recommendation he had presented. Mary, being astute and receptive to recommendations for quality dentistry, chose the fixed bridge option.

Unbelievably, at the moment Mary announced her decision to replace the removable type with a fixed bridge, Dr. Weyh's receptionist received a phone call informing her that the patient scheduled in 20 minutes would not be able to keep her appointment. The office had marked off close to two hours for that patient's procedure. Weyh, not wanting to sit for the next two hours, took a chance and told Mary, a healthy and vital 70 year old, he could begin her work immediately....if she had the time. She readily accepted and asked him to get started.

To say Fred Weyh was pleased with how the events had worked out would be like saying a new car salesman is slightly smiling as a prospective buyer pulls his checkbook out after a brief look at the show room car. Fred, quite literally, was delighted.

He hit the position switch on the dental chair, moving Mary to full recline, and then proceeded with donning each of the now ever-present OSHA "trademark items" for dentists....the face mask over his nose and mouth, the plastic face and eye shield and, of course, his operating gloves. His patient's response, as she watched him "suit up" was, **"Oh, Doctor, I do hope it's a *boy* this time!"**

—*Submitted by: Fred J. Weyh, D.D.S.*
Kearny, AZ

"I GOT LONG ROOTS, DOC....!"

*T*his next story, submitted by Alan M. Novich, is a beautiful example of someone's literal interpretation and belief in the maxim, "*you pay extra for quality.*" In this case, the someone happened to be Geraldo Estavez, one of New York City's "upper ghetto resident sharpies."

Geraldo had seen Dr. Novich on a prior visit to have an abscessed upper left second molar removed. At that visit, he had been accompanied by his brother, Cesar, and had left the office with a deep sense of confidence and satisfaction with the care rendered by "Doctor Alan." He sang Alan's praises, literally, for months following his extraction and had even been a steady source of referrals for the office.

"Dr. Novich, I bet you'll never guess who's waiting to see you," Alan's receptionist baited him, one snowy Wednesday morning in late December.

"Winston Churchill....he's freshly resurrected and has an erupting fourth molar! Right?" Alan answered,

in his inimitable way.

"Seriously, Dr. Novich, it's that little guy, Geraldo Estavez. From what I can tell, he has a terrific tooth-ache. Shall I seat him now?"

"You bet. Don't dare make the **best referral source in the ghetto** wait one second longer than absolutely necessary!"

Alan Novich entered the operatory where Geraldo had been seated, and there, in an 8 x 10 room, was his patient....dressed to the nines and surrounded by an en-tourage of six characters who would make most of us do a little quiver and quake number....especially if we met them in the subway after dark.

However, Dr. Novich, being the popular figure he had become in the area, recognized the frightening sight before him was no cause for fear....thanks to the reputa-tion Geraldo and Cesar had helped establish for him.

"Hey, man, there he is," Geraldo said, as Alan en-tered the room. "The doc who took out my last tooth without it hurtin at all. Hey, Doc! What's happening, man?"

"Oh, the same old grind, Geraldo. Great to see you

again! You got a bad one, do you?" Alan asked as he shook hands with Geraldo.

"I'm telling you, man! This baby's almost taken me out, Doc!" he said, as he pointed to the left side of his lower jaw.

"Bobbi, get Vicky to take a quick x-ray and let's see what's going on," Dr. Novich instructed his longtime assistant, as he eyed the crowd of characters huddled around the dental chair. He *smiled*, when he told them they might be more comfortable in the waiting room.

"Hey, Doc, no way! These guys need to see how great you are with those pliers. They're okay. Don't worry about them, man, these dudes are used to standing."

Alan Novich knew enough about these types to simply drop it. For that matter, he thought to himself, 'they can assist me if that's what they want to do.'

"Oh, you've got it developed already, Vicky. Thanks. This is a nice film!" Alan said, as he held the film up to the lighted view box for a better look.

The x-ray showed a lower left first premolar without a stitch of bone around it, a classic case of advanced periodontal (gum) disease. Upon doing his clinical exam, Dr. Novich found the tooth was **flapping in the breeze**, as we dentists are prone to say when a tooth has absolutely no bone support around it. Actually, the only thing holding this tooth in the patient's mouth was the gum tissue around it. Miraculously, the tooth had somehow not already fallen out.

"Geraldo, the tooth needs to come out, and it looks pretty loose," Novich said.

"Great Doc! Now, tell me how much it's gonna set me back....!"

"Thirty bucks."

"**Thirty bucks?** Doc, you must have forgotten who's in your chair!" Geraldo responded, obviously unhappy with what he'd just been told.

At that moment, the staff, even Alan himself, might have given in to a little uncertainty about the next thing to be said, had not Geraldo quickly followed with a vehement protest....

"But, Doc, I'm warnin' you, *I got long roots, man!* You must have forgotten since that last time, huh? *It ain't gonna come out easy*, I don't care what the x-ray say. I know, man!"

"Okay," Novich replied, **"fifty bucks, then!!"**

"Now, that's more like it, Doc," Geraldo replied with a big smile. "Get on with it, man! I know *it ain't no way you gonna cause me no pain for fifty bucks!!!"*

—*Submitted by:* Alan M. Novich, Attorney at Law
New York, NY

"A PECKERWOOD STRIKES A....."

*I*n certain parts of the country, particularly in the southern states, there is a word, not flattering and more commonly used when I was a boy than it is today, that denotes an individual with little formal education, culture or awareness and concern for the social amenities or graces. The word...peckerwood! Today, the word more appropriate for this descriptive intent would be....redneck.

Either word, for purposes of this story, would be accurate in personifying the patient seen by Dr. Sam A. Marascalco some 40 years ago in the little town of Grenada, Ms. The words are of the same genre'.... "a rose by any other name!"

"Dr. Sam," as I affectionately and respectfully refer to my uncle, is now retired in Tucson. He has often been described as a dentist's dentist, due to the extraordinary excellence of his work. Besides being a wonderful dentist, he has always been, by anyone's measurements, a gentleman. Cultured, considerate to a fault.

The antithesis of a peckerwood....or redneck.

I know him to have such a vigilance of conscience that he would never have used the disparaging word "peckerwood" when describing the event I am about to unfold. It is strictly my interpretation of the report, given by his lifetime office manager and sister, Dona Marascalco, that caused me to use this sobriquet.

Now, having a sense of the professional and personality profile of the dentist in this story, let me describe the dental equipment used some 30 to 40 years ago. It is crucial to the core of this account. Most of the units had a cuspidor integrally attached. On the older units, there was also a round porcelain bracket table upon which the dentist placed his hand instrumentation.

With this background on the dentist and the equipment of that day, let me present Mr. "Red Pruitt," the patient. Oh, mea culpa, one more obligatory and salient digression....99 percent of all peckerwoods seem to have the disgusting habit of either dipping snuff or chewing tobacco. Usually, both! It is almost axiomatic that the individual must indulge in at least one of these pursuits before a valid ordination of the title peckerwood or redneck can be conferred.

Red Pruitt, a "walk-in" patient, was a "registered peckerwood," his title confirmed by the snuff leaking down the corners of his mouth as he walked into the office and by the description of his "emergency problem" to Miss Dona.

"I nees my teef kleened and cheked. My toofs hav bin a'bothin me fer sum time now, and since it shore a nuf don't apeers this here a'rainin is gonna let me git in them thar fields to plow, and all, I's sot my mind up to go a'hed and git my toofs seen bout. Can yore toof docter see bout me this here mownin?" he asked Dona, in his pure peckerwood elocution.

"Well, we usually take patients by appointment only, but let me see if Dr. Sam can work you in.." she responded. "Are you in pain?" Dona asked, with the family grace she innately possessed, knowing her brother was booked for the morning but, also aware he would always see a patient in pain.

"Yassam, this here toof has a'bin thobbin fur might near two or three weeks I spect. It's a'specially bad at nite time. I bleve it's a'done swol up on me up this mownin."

True to character, Sam told Dona to have his assistant seat the patient in an available chair. First, Dona, with great patience and persistence, assisted Pruitt with his health history questionnaire. The short of it being that "Red" knew very little about his medical background and had never ever been to a dentist during 47 years on this planet. Thank God for rain and an abscess....Huh?

Dr. Sam introduced himself to the patient with a warm and comforting smile, his big blue eyes transferring no judgement or indictment of the patient's lifelong remiss of his dentition. They did see, instantly, the narrow brown trail of snuff residue in the crease of skin, extending from the corner of the patient's mouth to the angle of his chin. Still, he only asked the professional questions needed for deducing the cause of the man's pain, and then proceeded with his clinical exam.

When "Red Pruitt" opened his mouth, the condition of his oral environment even took this dentist with World War II experience aback. His teeth were covered with snuff, tobacco, some 47 years of calculus buildup (the hard, chalky looking material which builds up on teeth between cleaning appointments), and the residue of onions, butter beans, and the other food he'd eaten the evening before. This was before face masks and gloves were standard protocol!

Sam, picking up his air-water syringe, advised the patient he was going to spray water in his mouth. His obvious plan was to wash the teeth off, in order to actually see what else might be lurking in there besides the snuff and food debris mentioned. The onion breath, Dr. Sam stoically stifled, somehow, from running the course of his olfactory nerve to the big transformer, where, if the smell had reached his brain, would have, no doubt, caused him to succumb to what most mere mortal dentists would have....a severe case of nausea. He did not. Probably another reason why his sister, Dona, often refers to him as, "A saint of a man, Joe."

"Mr. Pruitt, I'm going to spray some water in your mouth. Would you please spit out when you're ready."

When Pruitt's mouth was as full of water as he could stand, before choking, Sam told him to empty his mouth. The patient then quite suddenly and unexpectedly, jumped up from the chair and spit the entire contents of his mouth, not in the cuspidor, but all over the instrument laden bracket table....

"Good gawd, Doc, you ain't a'plannin on a'puttin them thar tools back in my mouf after I's just spit all that thar shit on em', ere ya now?"

Dr. Marascalco's only reaction and reply, according to those who were there, was: "That will be all for today, Mr. Pruitt...." He left the room, shaking his head, but with a smile....The peckerwood had struck....a saint!

—*Reported by:* Dona V. Marascalco
Office manager, retired
Tucson, AZ

"A ONE TRACK MIND....?"

*D*r. Barbara Pampalone, a California dentist, was delivering a new complete denture on a middle-aged male whose health-history questionnaire indicated his work was heavy construction. He was a robust, no frills sort of guy. The only thing giving away his obvious out-of-shape physical condition was the size of his beer belly. Otherwise, the musculature of his upper torso caused him to resemble a slightly overweight middle linebacker for some pro football team.

Barbara, after seating the denture in the patient's mouth, immediately informed him....

"Look, Mike, I'm leaving town this afternoon for an *implant* session. I won't be back for two days. If you feel like there are going to be some sore spots, please, for God's sake, try to identify them now. I'd like to eliminate any potential trouble, now, before I leave, because I'm going to really be into *my implant thing* for a full 48 hours...in fact, I'm long overdue on taking care of this....."

Mike looked up, rolled his eyes, and drawled....

"Doc, please don't bother me with your *sexual* problems!"

—*Submitted by:* B.R. Pampalone, D.D.S.
Chatsworth, CA

"CLOSER TO THE PHONE....PLEASE!"

I have a number of "favorite dental stories" in this book, and this has to be one of them. I think one reason is the obvious similarity between the personality of the dentist in this story, and myself. We have, as they say, about the same boiling point....

Dr. Phillip J. Cato (not real name) received a phone call around 10 p.m., about the time he usually was getting ready for bed. The call came from the husband of a lady whom he had seen two weeks earlier. She had been seen to cement a completed porcelain veneer crown on her upper left central incisor (a front tooth). It was clear, from the moment he answered the phone, the man was irate. Inebriation was also a distinct possibility.

"Dr. Cato, this is William Stanley. You put a crown on my wife's front tooth, and I think the shape and color is all wrong!" He didn't bother with the amenities, choosing rather to attack him from the get go.

Phil Cato attempted to explain to the guy that his wife, like all patients he treated for cosmetic work, was given a mirror and ample time to evaluate the crown before it was cemented. He tried to convey to the angry husband his office policy of offering to place the crown with temporary cement for a few days, in order to give the patient time to be sure he or she is satisfied with the work. He went on to say Mrs. Stanley had actually gone on and on about how much she liked the crown and saw no reason to place it temporarily. She had been quite firm in asking Dr. Cato to place it with final type cement.

As Cato continued to try and get across to the surly and unreasonable husband, his wife had left the office visibly pleased with the work....he was interrupted again and again. He even tried to make the point that the man's wife had been told to call the office if she had any problems whatsoever, but, to his knowledge, she had never called with a complaint.

Finally, after at least a half dozen interruptions during the course of Dr. Cato defending himself, the patient loudly blurted out with, "My God, man, can't you see the damn color is all wrong?"

At this point, Cato was where gunpowder ignites....a spark, and there it goes!! He had tried to be so nice, so reassuring and professional. But, now, with these words, he went off....

"Well, I tell you what, if you will hold the son-of-a-bitching crown closer to the phone, maybe I can see what a lousy shade match I made!!!"

Postscript: The man hung up and the wife never mentioned the incident on any of her subsequent re-call visits to the office....either too embarrassed or un-aware of what her husband had done.

—*Submitted by*: David V. Haning, D.D.S.
Shinniston, WV

"CHRISTMAS GOODIES"

Thomas R. Kuhn, a young dentist who began his practice in San Francisco, shortly after the Summer of Love, was beginning to enjoy the fruits and gifts of his patients' love and appreciation. This was especially true during the Christmas season, when they would bring in cakes, cookies and pastries of all assortments. It was a time, as attested to by many dentists who went into practice during the late '60s and early '70s, when patients seemed more appreciative, more attached to "their doctors." The love and peace from the mid year of '67, when it started to reach the zenith of its unique lifespan, seemed to slide, softly and sweetly, into those years immediately following that now long vanished summer. It was the salad days of so many of us, now in our early- to mid-fifties.

One patient brought young Dr. Kuhn a plate full of delicious smelling brownies right before Christmas, 1969. His assistant placed the brownies in the back room which was beginning to look like a bakery. Dr.

Kuhn, like any live dentist, had **a secret sweet tooth**. He managed to munch, in no time at all, three or four of the brownies before seeing his next patient, a lady scheduled for a full gold crown preparation. He told his staff they were absolutely delicious!

About 30 to 40 minutes after inhaling the brownies, he was at the point where dentists place a string-like cord around the crown preparation, in order to retract the soft tissue before taking the impression of the tooth. Quite suddenly, and with no prior symptomology, Thomas pulled his head back from the patient, shook it a time or two, and said to his patient and assistant....

"Would you ladies excuse me a moment please....?" he said, as he stood up from the chair and started out of the operatory towards his private office.

Kuhn made no more than five steps down the hallway, when he knew something was seriously wrong....the carpet seemed to undulate underneath his unsteady feet, everything seemed like it was in slow motion, even his receptionist's voice, which sounded like it was echoing out of a deep well, as she asked:

"Dr. Kuhn, are you okay? You look really weird!"

Her words did something else....he started to giggle and feel silly. A few more minutes and Thomas realized he was high as a kite....stoned....on **"Alice B. Toklas' Brownies."**

Gathering composure, he returned to the operatory and somehow, managed to get a temporary crown on the tooth. He apologetically explained to his patient, and assistant, he was high on marijuana and in no condition to continue the procedure. At first disbelieving her dentist would be doped on grass, the patient began to laugh. With that, Thomas really took on the giggles....

Clearly seeing "her doctor" was stoned, the lady decided a retreat from the office was in her best interest. She bid adieu to Dr. Kuhn, but assured him she would reschedule.....after listening to more profuse apologies and his explanation about the brownies that had taken a bite out of his brain. Minutes after the patient left the office, Thomas decided he should take the afternoon off! The staff unanimously agreed and gave their assurances **they would leave him a few of the brownies....to eat on the week-end!**

—*Submitted by:* Thomas R. Kuhn, D.M.D.
San Francisco, CA

"ROOT CANALS....CAN HURT!!!!!"

*T*ndividuals, in life's game of solitaire, oftentimes deal some portion of their fate, as the cards of place and circumstance come up, at a certain moment in time.

The place....my dental office. A place, naturally, full of dental equipment. Equipment which always functions with German-like perfection while in warranty. However, the day the warranty of parts and labor expires, the equipment begins to behave like a 20 year old Jaguar.....either broken, or breaking down at the moment it's needed most!

The circumstances....my tendency to procrastinate "calling the service rep" ($40 to $50 per hour, plus parts and/or "loaner fees"). First, I try to "fix" the malfunctioning equipment, or resurrect it if it's acting like it's dead. Then, if I cannot, I "let it ride for a while"....if it's simply a "nuisance" type of problem and not one which altogether makes me "dead in the water."

Continuing with this "self-imposed" rendezvous

with fate's heavy hand, the circumstances centered around *a relay switch* which would not shut off. Without being too technical, my dental unit has its instrument tray designed so each of the high and low speed handpieces (the drills) is cradled off the edge of the tray, in its own separate hard plastic sleeve. When not being used, the relay cuts off power to that handpiece. This is done to keep it from continuing to run and spray water while another handpiece is being used in the patient's mouth.

So, my relay wouldn't cut off when the pencil-like handpiece was placed in its cradle. I could cut it off by flipping the switch to "off" for that particular one. **Sometimes, I forgot!** When I did, it started running, at better than 100,000 rpm, and would spray water everywhere each time I stepped on the floor rheostat (like a car's gas pedal, it allows electrical power and air to cause the handpiece to drill)!

Now, I'm working on a guy from Valparaiso, Indiana. A mix of Santa Claus and Will Rogers, Sr. A jolly "never met a stranger sort of fellow." **A wonderful human being!** A man who had unquestioned faith in my manual dexterity skills and coordination, until the day

I was reassuring him, on and on, there was no pain to expect from a root canal he was to undergo later that day by a specialist....

"But, Joe, what about when they start drilling into the nerve tissue itself?" he asked. Again, I reassured him and then....

Accidentally, while standing, I stepped on my foot control with the heel of my foot and drilled a hole....the size of a 701 bur (about 1/16th to 1/8 th of an inch long)....right into my rear end!!! Man, did I let out an "OUCH"....the actual word, I believe, was "SON-OF-A-BITCH....THAT HURT!!!!"

Chuck Adams, after discerning what caused my un-expected exclamation, was slow and steady with his ver-balizing:

"Damn, Joe....I believe you just did a root canal on your right cheek, huh?"

—*Submitted by:* The author
Jackson, MS

"THE WHITE MAN'S WEIRD MEDICINE"

*D*uring the '70s, Dr. Richard Haag was the dental director for a private hospital at Gando on the Navaho Indian Reservation in northern Arizona.

One autumn afternoon, while working past 5 p.m. on some of that day's patient charts, he heard a soft knock at the front door. There, with one hand cupped over her right cheek, was a Navaho woman. Dick didn't speak Navaho and the woman didn't speak English, but this was irrelevant since the hand on the cheek explained the problem in mankind's universal language.

Haag led the hurting patient back to the operatory, seated her, clinically examined her teeth, and took an x-ray of the tooth suspected of causing the problem. He went ahead and anesthetized the area with a local anesthetic (gave her a shot), then tried to explain to his patient he was going back to the front office but would return in a few minutes. The patient nodded as if she understood.

Dick Haag went back to the front desk where he finished writing on the patient charts about 10 minutes later. He got up from the desk, tidied things up a bit, turned off the lights, and walked out of the clinic....locking the door behind him.

Dr. Haag's apartment was about the equivalent of a city block from the dental clinic, and he usually enjoyed a leisurely stroll home after putting in a hard day at the office. Frequently, as with this late afternoon walk to his apartment, he stopped along the way and chatted with acquaintances.

Arriving home, he unlocked his door, entered the kitchen, and it hit him like a ton of bricks....he'd locked his patient in the darkened dental clinic!!! He immediately ran out of the apartment, raced back down the street to the clinic, unlocked the front door, turned on the lights and rushed back to see how the woman was doing....fully expecting to see a terror-stricken patient.

There, sitting composed and quite comfortable....in total darkness....was the Indian woman. After flipping the light switch and making futile attempts at apologizing and explanations, Dr. Haag realized she wasn't going to comprehend, so he simply proceeded with extraction of the very, very numb tooth.

After the extraction, he dismissed the patient, again desperately trying to convey post extraction home-care instructions in English. The patient simply smiled....

Several weeks later Dr. Haag learned through an interpreter that the patient had returned home and reinforced to her family that the white man's medicine was indeed strong, if not quite weird. In her paraphrased words, she said:

"To stop tooth from hurting, white man first stick sharp needle in mouth, then make room total dark and silent...in short while tooth stop hurting and white man return to take bad tooth away....!"

—*Submitted by:* Richard Haag, D.D.S.
Flagstaff, AZ

"IN DEATH, THEY SHALL NOT PART...."

The patient waiting to see Dr. Pampalone was an elderly gentleman...

Dr. Pampalone had just left her very professional C.D.A. (certified dental assistant) in the next room laughing, but refusing to say what was so funny about the man whom she had just left to come and get Dr. Pampalone....

"You just go talk to him!" her assistant said, as Dr. Pampalone walked out of the room. "You'll see."

Barbara Pampalone greeted the gentleman and, though she was not given to spotting habits, she had a strong suspicion of being in the presence of a still indulging alcoholic.

He was wearing an old, ill-fitting upper denture and had the remnants of six lower front teeth, the roots still there only because the heavily diseased gum tissue had not yet turned loose of them. Bone support was non existent. The man was wearing no lower partial denture, and when she realized that, she was half-irritated with her prized assistant. She couldn't comprehend anything funny about a situation as pitiful as this one.

"You say there is no pain with the teeth?" she asked the old guy.

"Nope, not a bit, Doc! But, I definitely want you to take these teeth out."

"But, if I remove them, you will need a lower denture made in order to properly chew your food. Believe it or not, what you have left is better than taking them out and then not replacing them with a denture. Your upper denture already seems to have some pretty significant problems. Are you ready to have a new upper and lower denture made at this time?" Dr. Pampalone inquired.

"Well, not really, Doctor."

"I don't understand."

"Well, you see, I had this friend....and, well, **sometimes we would trade teeth and you know, Doc, his teeth seemed to fit me better than my own teeth....**"

"Remarkable!"

"Yeah, it's like this, Doc....he had a lower denture, too. And, well, my friend up and died recently, *so I want you to take these here snags out so I can start wearing his lower denture with his upper denture, which is what I'm wearing right now.*"

"I headed for the adjacent operatory, throwing my hands into the air as I joined my assistant!" Dr. Pampalone reminisced..

"I see you talked to him, Doctor," the assistant said, a moment before they grabbed each other and started howling.

—*Submitted by:* B.K. Pampalone, D.D.S.
Chatsworth, CA

"Just pretend I'm a straw...."

*H*ygienists, as a group, confirmed by 26 years of personally working very close to a significant number of them and interpretation of many of the reports I've received while writing this book, seem to have *a devilish-like penchant for sometimes saying the opposite of what they intend to convey.* I'm not saying this is endemic, heaven forbid, no, but I am confirming that a general tendency does exist. Let me present another example of this phenomenon....

Lyn Donovan, the hygienist who gave us the "*expectorate story*" also, rather magnanimously, tells one on herself. It seems, according to Lyn's own admission, she possesses an insidious imp which makes her, periodically, say the wrong things to her patient.... **"It's like the wrong words just sometimes jump right out of my mouth, and I don't know where they came from."**

One afternoon, close to the point of actually completing work on the patient in her chair, she, like always, began to fill his mouth with water from the air-

water syringe prior to placing in the high-speed evacuation tip and suctioning out the accumulated water and debris. Instead of the usual and customary instructions to the patient coming out of her mouth (how to put his lips around the tip "like you do when sucking on a straw"), the devil, or something, made her say, **"Okay, Bob, just put your lips around me and suck!!"**

—*Submitted by:* Lyn Donovan,
Cerritos, CA

"BLEACH 'EM OR BOIL 'EM?...."

The patient had, somehow, misplaced his upper denture, and after a frantic, but fruitless search, reclassified his false teeth from "temporarily misplaced" to "fully lost." When he reached the point where he thought further searching was to no avail, he called the "dental champion" of this story—Dr. David V. Haning.

Dr. Haning had reached the stage in construction of the new denture, where the teeth are in wax and ready for try-in, when he received an unexpected phone call....

"Doc, this is Ralph Jansen...you know the guy you're making the new denture for?"

"Sure, Ralph. Of course....I've actually got them ready for you to try in."

"Well, Doc....hell, I hate to tell you this. But, look, I found my old dentures this morning. I need you to stop work on those new ones, please!"

"Why that's wonderful, Ralph...." David Haning said, not wanting to sound upset or put out with the lucky patient. "But, you don't sound like a man who's just found out he's going to save several hundred dollars. Are they in one piece?" Haning asked after denoting a tone in the patient's voice which indicated something was not just right.

"Doc, I'm glad you asked....uh, there is a slight problem, and I....uh, I don't know how to tell you this..."

"What is it Mr. Jansen?" David solicitously asked. "I'm sure I can help with whatever might be the problem."

Like many dentures which have been lost, then found, he reasoned they could have been chipped or lost a tooth or two during the period of time the patient had lost track of them....

'Heck, I still might get a denture repair or tooth replacement out of this deal,' Dr. Haning thought to himself. I mean, after all, he had invested several hours of chairside time to the guy's new dentures, not to mention a commercial lab bill....it wouldn't be wrong to think about a little compensation, instead of a total bust on this case.

"Well, Doc, actually what I need to know is...uh, what can I use to...uh, clean my dentures off before I put them back in my mouth? My wife said *Listerine*, but I'm not sure that will be good enough. I was...uh, thinking maybe about *Clorox*, or something like that....you know, uh, *something that might kill some of those bad kind of germs*, and all, but I wasn't sure if bleach would hurt the plate or not...uh, what do you think, Doc?"

David Haning knew, without holding a doctorate in psychology, his patient's denture must be dirty, real dirty, and he was reluctant to put them back in his mouth, certainly not without first discussing it with his dentist.

"What kind of *stain* is on the denture, Mr. Jansen?" Haning inquired, naturally assuming, with all the stuttering and stammering, the denture had something quite visible adhering to its surface.

"Doc, its not really a stain."

"Not a stain, you say, Mr. Jansen?"

"Not a stain, Doc. Right! They're not stained...."

"Then why did you ask about Clorox, a bleach, if

they're not stained?" the dentist asked, his curiosity now growing over an apparent mystery his patient seemed about as willing to reveal as a large mouth bass is to spit out a juicy minnow.

"Where did you find your denture, Mr. Jansen? David now asked, hoping to cut straight through the mysterious mist.

"Actually.....uh, well, I'll tell you this, Doc....I didn't find the dentures. Someone else did."

"Who found the teeth, Mr. Jansen?"

"My plumber.....my plumber found them, Doc. That's who found them.....my plumber!!!!" the patient said, sounding like someone who has just confessed to a long-hidden and heinous crime against man and God.

"Where did he find them, Ralph?"

"Some pipes were stopped up, Doc. He....uh, un-stopped some pipes and found them there. That's why I'm wondering about the germ thing and all....you un-derstand what I'm saying Doc?"

"Well, not exactly," Haning replied, "exactly where did he......?"

"IN THE GOSH-DAMN TOILET!!!!!" the

patient interrupted before Dr. Haning could complete the question. "Yeah, that's right, Doc, in the damn toilet!"

"Have you put them in your mouth, yet?"

"Are you crazy, Doc? Why in the hell do you think I'm calling?" Jansen now asked, with confession now fortifying his voice with an anger not heard before the disclosure.

The dentist understood the sudden switch from halting, hesitation of speech, to this tone was simply symptomatic of the patient's own disgust at where his teeth had been and where they would be as soon as he found something appropriate enough to sterilize, if you will, the very thought itself...the very knowledge and confession of his teeth having been trapped in the bottom of the toilet pipes.

"Ralph, Clorox will be too caustic. It will actually take all the color out of the pink part of your denture...."

"How about boiling them, Doc?" he interrupted again.

"Not boiling, no. It will distort the denture base. They'll never fit again...."

"Damn, Doc, what then? Surely you guys know something about how to clean up dentures when they've been in.....

"Actually, no, Mr. Jansen," David broke in for the first time since the now extended conversation had begun. *"Really, I've never had a patient tell me his denture has been in the....uh, in the toilet. I guess we could...."*

"Doc, forget it, please!" Jansen blurted out. "Forget it, I need you to finish the work on that new denture. You and I both know that this old denture always gave me trouble. **It's not that they were in the....in the damn toilet!!!!"**

Postscript: How's that for justifying money for a "new denture," not to mention helping a patient make the decision, huh?

—*Submitted by:* David V. Haning, D.D.S.
Shinniston, WV

"A CASE OF CAT SCRATCH FEVER"

A teenage boy was referred into the base dental clinic, the same U.S.A.F. dental facility where the lady was radiographed with an antenna sticking out of her skull, and this time the referral was made by the ENT department instead of the family practice group. The boy's consultation form requested a dental examination to possibly determine the cause of a large, submandibular swelling (swelling under the angle of the lower jaw). The consultation form did specify that the boy's medical evaluation had found him to be within normal limits.

The attending dentist did a clinical intraoral examination (looked into the patient's mouth for evidence of any abnormalities or problems), along with a full x-ray survey of his dentition. Both were negative. An oral pathologist was then called in on the case, since both the medical and dental examination had proven inconclusive in determining the patient's problem. The pathologist, upon initial examination of the teenager, immediately noted a scratch behind his left ear, and quite perceptively, the residue of cat hair on his T-shirt. His presumptive diagnosis, quite naturally, was a case of Cat Scratch Fever.

The pathologist completed the consultation form and returned it to the E.N.T. department with the following message:

"Dental examination complete, as requested. Patient is also dentally within normal limits...please evaluate T-shirt."

—*Submitted by:* William T. Nelly, III, D.M.D.
Plattsburgh, N.Y.

"THE FOREIGN CURRENCY"

Thirty-five year old David Donald Nelson had been in practice with his father for three years when he learned a lesson about financial discussions which forever changed his attitude about collections for his dental services....

Dr. Nelson had presented a comprehensive plan of treatment to his patient, Mary, several weeks earlier, when she called to discuss his "flexibility on payment options." David, like many dentists, took to heart his patient's detailed and dreary financial condition. Against his better judgment, and the office policy which clearly spelled out the payment plans available, he reluctantly agreed to go ahead with extraction of one of her painful teeth after she made an offer to make "a partial cash payment and something else....." The patient had to also give her assurance of taking the course of antibiotics he had prescribed.

When the patient arrived for her appointment a

week later, the tooth was quickly removed without complications. She profusely thanked Dr. Nelson for expertly removing the chronically abscessed tooth and, for being understanding about her financial picture....

"Oh, Dr. David, thank you so much for making special arrangements for me. I'll go to the car right now and fetch my payment," Mary said, as she left the operatory with a big grin.

A few minutes later, Dr. Nelson was in consultation with his next patient when he heard a shrill shriek from the direction of his business manager's office. It sounded, the best he could tell, like the voice of Debbie, the office manager. Not hearing the sound a second time, and not wanting to appear like anything was amiss, for the sake of his patient's confidence, he continued to work. About 15 minutes later, at an obvious breaking point with his patient's treatment, David stopped and went to investigate the earlier vocal outburst....

"Debbie, was that you I heard a few minutes ago?" David asked his business manager.

"It certainly was, Dr. Nelson!" Debbie replied in an emphatic tone. "Do you know what that crazy woman paid you for taking that tooth out?"

"Well, my understanding was that she would make a partial cash payment, today, along with s*ome type of foreign currency....*"

"What kind of *currency* did you say, Doctor?" Debbie asked with a quizzical grimace.

"Foreign currency of some kind.. I'm really not sure. *Rhode Island* something or other. I really didn't understand her at the time....I just felt sorry for the lady and agreed. She did say she would make regular cash payments, along with the other stuff."

"**Dr. Nelson, do you know anything at all about chickens?**"

"**Nothing except that they lay eggs and can be fried, barbecued, baked or broiled. Why do you ask, Debbie?**"

"Because your last patient paid you with a $10 bill, U.S. minted currency, and two *Rhode Island Red baby chickens!*"

"**Paid me with what?**" David asked, completely surprised with what he had just heard.

"You heard me right. Ten dollars and two chirping chickens. Yep, that was me you heard scream. I've seen a lot of payment plans in my day, Dr. Nelson, but this one takes the cake. Did you seriously not know what a Rhode Island Red was....?"

Before the conversation could go further, David Nelson abruptly turned and left the business office to complete his treatment on the patient in his chair. He was obviously embarrassed and didn't feel like defending the naivete' of his city upbringing at this point in time.

Debbie, being the ever dutiful and improvising employee, had quickly sequestered the baby chicks in the staff lounge soon after their sudden and unexpected appearance on her desk. It might have solved the immediate problem had there not been a very efficient central air and heating duct system in the office....

All throughout the remainder of the day, one patient after another asked Drs. Paul and David Nelson what the *strange sounds and smell* were in the office. Fortunately, close to the end of the day, one of the assistants, Ann, offered to take the chicks out to her grandfather's farm. Young Dr. Nelson made no protest to the offer.

Before actually leaving the office with the "chirping currency," it was agreed that the male chick would be named David, and his mate, Betty Jo, after the dental auxiliary who had assisted David at the time of Mary's extraction procedure.

Aftermath: Ann periodically brought pictures of her and Dr. David's adopted offspring. The two Rhode Island Reds had grown, in a matter of months, into a large and flourishing family. A local radio station had picked up the story, somehow, and their morning announcer had called the office around 9 a.m. one day and unknowing to David Nelson, D.M.D., placed him on the air...the gist of which was to let the listeners know about this dentist who entertained unusual payment options. **To date, Dr. Nelson has not accepted any more chickens in lieu of monetary payment...only as patients.**

—*Submitted by:* David D. Nelson, D.M.D.
Tuscaloosa, AL

"ACHTUNG IN THE CHAIR"

An elementary comprehension and appreciation for the military chain of command is essential for this next story....

Fundamentally, a basic training military recruit is the lowest level of the chain of command. From there, everything is up! After recruit, the chain goes something like this...private, corporal, sergeant, lieutenant, captain (rank which dentists and physicians usually come into the service), major, colonel, and on up to a five star general....the highest military rank.

The previous breakdown is not as precise as one could be, since there are different levels, within a certain rank. For instance, an officer could be designated a "light colonel" or a "full colonel." But, for the purposes of this report, this is the rank structure of our system.

The most important thing to understand, before tasting the full flavor of humor in another Ron Kunz story, is that *orders....given from any rank above, must be obeyed!* This is the way of the military, and if it were any other way, then it would have crumbled before now. Orders, when given and blindly obeyed, are the essence of winning wars. It has to be as rigidly adhered to on the sidewalks of a military base back in the states, as it is on a distant battlefield....

Ron, an army dentist from 1966-68, had a basic training recruit in his chair one day while at Fort Dix, New Jersey. Since Dr. Kunz had captain stripes, this little guy was really giving him the "yes-sirs and no-sirs." He responded, quite formally, to anything Ron said or asked. After placing the amalgam (silver) filling, Kunz was preparing to check the recruit's occlusion (his bite) with the blue articulating paper, when he told him, *"Okay, close down and move back and forth."*

The young recruit immediately closed his mouth and wiggled his butt back and forth in the chair!

—*Submitted by:* Ron A. Kunz, D.M.D.
Pittsburgh, PA

"JESSICA"

"Our office belongs to a referral service. One day they called to say they were referring a multiple personality patient. Eventually, a middle-aged woman came in for an examination and told me, during my history taking, she suffered from a multiple-personality disorder. After she made that statement, I don't believe I heard another word. All I could think about was why had I been so damn lucky. Later, after I settled down, I began to actually consider treating her...more out of curiosity, I'm sure, than compassion.

However, before treating her, I did have the presence of mind to phone her psychiatrist for information and advice. He informed me this patient was capable of regressing into the personality of a young girl whose name was Jessica. He went on to tell me, in a clear tone of warning, to never schedule her as the last patient of the day. I asked why, and he answered by saying if she should experience a personality change while I was treating her, it would most likely keep me late into the evening....waiting for her to revert to an adult."

"What triggers her regression into the Jessica personality?" I asked the psychiatrist.

"Any type of stress can precipitate the transformation!" was his immediate reply.

'Oh, great! Dentistry never stresses patients,' I thought, with a sick laugh to myself.

"Well, on the day of treatment, in she came with a teddy bear in her hands. She was still clearly the adult, but it didn't take a genius to figure out she was probably on the edge of becoming Jessica. I was gentle as possible throughout the dental procedure, but I had the distinct feeling this lady did not like me....or, perhaps, men in general! Then, before I could say Sigmund Freud, she transferred to the Jessica personality. I asked her who she was and she affirmed, in a little girl's voice, she was Jessica! You've heard of sweating bullets, browning out, cold sweat. Yes, I was simultaneously experiencing all of these. And, to make matters worse, she was the last patient of the day!

We completed treatment, but she remained the little girl, Jessica. She then insisted, after realizing we had finished our work, on getting out of the chair and driving herself home. Yes, folks, in a 10- year-old voice, Jessica was becoming adamant about leaving in her car. A clear thinking assistant, Pam, snatched the car keys from her open purse, as Jessica hit the front door. Trying to hold back my hysterics, I phoned her psychiatrist and asked him what to do. He indicated, after hearing the details, that we should put her in her car, where she would fall asleep, and then throw her keys into the back seat. He assured me she would awaken later, in the adult personality, find her keys, somehow, and then drive home.

The staff and I rushed outside, but having no idea what her car looked like, began trying the keys in every car in the parking lot. *I felt like a car thief and knew, any minute, I'd be arrested.* Besides not knowing her car, we had no idea where she was...by this time our runaway emotions mercifully came to a stop. I was now angry! I went back inside the clinic and phoned the patient's home to inform her, on an answering machine, just how mad I was for her doing this to us. I went on to tell her she could pick her keys up the next day....

The next day she came in as the adult person asking for her keys as if nothing had happened, and, before leaving, asked my receptionist to please make an appointment for a close friend of hers...a girl named Jamie! She asked for a 4 p.m. appointment!"

—*Submitted by:* Philip R. Jen Kin, D.D.S.
Cerritos, CA

"TOUGH AS LEATHER"

*T*he following came in from the "Wolverine State." So many crazy things seem to happen early on in one's dental career, as I mentioned in the opening remarks of this book. This story from a young Michigan dentist pretty much confirms my research findings. They remind me, in certain ways, of the numerous nutty episodes in my own early years of practice.

Arnold Weitenberner of Chesterfield Twp., Michigan, hadn't been out of dental school very long before his father "hit him up for some free dentistry." In all fairness, I should say "some reimbursement towards all the financial assistance" provided by father Weitenberner during the undergraduate and dental school education of young Arnold. Actually, I'm almost positive his dad made the appointment because he knew, beyond a shadow of a doubt, his son was the *best dentist in the state of Michigan*, maybe in the U.S. Why, of course! How could it have had anything to do with money? Perish the thought!! Impossible! Right,

Mr. Weitenberner?

But, before going on, let me point out how absolutely amazing it is to observe the "relatives" who seem to materialize, out of the woodwork, whenever a young healthcare professional hangs up his or her shingle for the first time. I had relatives coming to me whose names I had never heard mentioned, at any time, by my immediate family. I used to think to myself, 'How in the hell can a *third cousin, of my mother's brother's wife,* be expecting me to see him on a Sunday....at a discounted fee?' Yes, almost to a 100%, they all wanted to be seen on "their day off," or Saturday or Sunday...my day out of the office, of course!

Now, I have no reason to believe Arnold's father was one of these kind of relatives. I mean, after all, a boy's father and mother ought to have some perks. One of those, according to Arnold, was his dad wanted some bragging rights about the great dentist his son had turned out to be. How else could the older Weitenberner get those rights, I ask you, without giving his son Arnold the "privilege" of doing some dental work for him. Right?

Okay....Arnold's father comes in for some routine

operative dentistry (placement of silver fillings), and leaves the office greatly impressed with his son's ability to administer an injection with no pain whatsoever, not even a twinge of pain with the needle!

Later that day, his father recalled to his golfing buddy, Frank Reiner, the details of his dental visit with "Junior." He went on and on about how smooth his boy was with the needle and all the instruments.... "I'm telling you, Frank," Weitenberner said, before going into the club house, "Arnold is one helluva dentist, if I say so myself. He's damn good, and you and Louise (Frank's wife) ought to really consider using him next time your recall cleaning is due. I've heard you badmouth old Doc Felix for years. Now's the time, Frank! Arnold's up on all the latest stuff. You need to keep that in mind!"

The latter dialogue might not be verbatim, admittedly, however, I'd wager *my vivid imagination* of the scenario is closer to the truth, than not. Anyway, suffice it to say Arnold's father was proud of his son being a dentist and had allowed him to restore some teeth he had been putting off until his son graduated and received his state licensure.....

....Again, I cannot help but tell you how many relatives wait...some actually die, waiting on physician kinfolk to finish training, while no small number have certainly lost teeth waiting until a son, daughter, nephew or niece completes dental school. Mr. Weitenberner was lucky—his son made it in time....

Anyway, Mr. and Mrs. Weitenberner, along with Arnold, his wife, and Frank and Louise Reiner, had dinner at the country club that evening. I understand Arnold's father and mother both ordered filet mignon, which was known for its savory tenderness. Arnold, his wife, and the Reiners ordered various dishes of baked and broiled fish. The usual conversations, during the course of a good meal with friends and relatives, was taking place when Arnold noticed his father apparently having some difficulty....

"Dad, is everything, okay?" Arnold asked his father.

"Well, actually, the meat seems a little tougher than usual. How's yours honey?" Mr. Weitenberner asked his wife.

"Mine is great darling.. Why don't you ask George (their waiter) to take yours back. You know he won't mind, dear!"

"Oh, I think not, hon. Hey, I'm fine, folks. The steak's great, I think I just hit a tough spot, there...."

After another 10 to 15 minutes of *gnawing, more like a dog on a good bone than a man chewing on a tender piece of filet mignon*, the older Weitenberner politely excused himself from the table....five minutes later he was back at the table, and devoured the remaining filet in less time than he had been gone.

On the way home, after they had parted company with the Reiners, Arnold noted, "Dad, you really seemed to be having a time with that steak back at the club. I sure am sorry the meat was so...."

"Actually, Arnold, it was like chewing a piece of leather til I pulled out those damn cotton rolls you left in there....

As the great bard said: "All's well that ends well." The next day, again on the golf course, Weitenberner was overheard telling his golfing buddy.... **"Frank, I'm telling you boy, it's sure hell trying to find a good dentist these days....You and Louise had better go ahead and do something!"**

—*Reported by:* Arnold Weitenberner, D.D.S.
Chesterfield Twp., MI

"OH, YES, WE STERILIZE....EVERYTHING!!!"

*I*n the paraphrased words of Dr. Philip R. Jen Kin, let me relate how well his office staff handles potentially embarrassing situations:

"We all (dentists) have cut out old fillings and had particles fall in the back of the patient's mouth. Try as hard as we can to gather all of them with the vacuum tip, the patient ends up retiring to the cuspidor or sink after the appointment and rinses out the remaining debris. This is no big deal! Right? Well, this particular day we had used a latch type slow-speed contra-angle handpiece (holds the bur in place) to remove decay in the teeth. At the base of the latch is a small screw that holds the latch to the rest of the handpiece....

We finished our appointment, the patient rinsed, we said our good-byes, and the patient went to the front desk to be reappointed. Our receptionist started to speak but noticed the patient had a quizzical look on his face. Shirley asked him if everything was okay, at which time he started to work his tongue around in his mouth...."

"Something feels weird in my mouth!" the patient said.

"Oh, it's probably a little piece of filling material," Shirley responded, with a little laugh.

The patient, just at the moment of Shirley's laugh, immediately flipped a small object out of his mouth, onto the counter top. Both heads immediately went down to more closely inspect the object. Yes, you guessed it, there was the tiny screw from the slow speed handpiece. Shirley, in an effort not to alarm the patient or sound like anything was out of the ordinary, said:

"Oh, yes, it's just what I thought....*thank you so much for hanging on to that*," Shirley said with a big smile as she picked the little screw up between her thumb and forefinger. "Here let me run this back to the Doctor right now......we must return each one of these for *autoclave sterilization*. I'll be back in a sec to make your next appointment," the fast-thinking receptionist said as she turned and quickly walked back toward the operatory.

Upon returning to her desk, Shirley found the patient a little wide-eyed and still moving his tongue around in his mouth...*perhaps in an attempt to reassure himself he had nothing else in his mouth....which should be returned for autoclave sterilization!*

"Thanks again for not throwing the instrument away!" Shirley said with a big smile, as she bid the patient good-bye. "Look forward to seeing you next week!"

Conclusion: By way of personal observation, it seems to me that Phil's receptionist is obviously *a class act and could probably increase her income, substantially, by putting on workshops for creative management of patients....*if a raise by him hasn't already cut off this potential for extra income.

—*Submitted by:* **Philip R. Jen Kin, D.D.S.**
Cerritos, CA

"Anything above the shoulders...."

*S*ince dentists and dental hygienists are given thorough anatomical instruction in the human head and neck area, particularly dentists, patients sometimes think of their field of expertise as being anything above the shoulders. If not the broad area, then certainly the mouth, teeth, and immediate surrounding structures....such as a patient's cheeks (facial)!

"I was finishing up a hygiene appointment with my polishing of the teeth. It was on a patient I had treated many times before," Lyn Donovan reports. "I glanced at her cheek and thought I spotted a light colored strand that my mind told me was a fiber from one of the 2 x 2 gauze pads I'd been using. I quickly grabbed it with my gloved thumb and first finger and pulled on it. The patient yelled and almost jumped out of the chair. Startled, myself, I immediately realized I had pulled out a solitary, long, white, facial hair! The patient, for some strange reason, had let it grow long on her face.

After my profuse apologizing, the patient, in an apparent attempt to lessen my embarrassment, responded with:"

"Yea, that was my wild hair, too! Everybody's got one, somewhere. But, don't you worry, honey, I won't be angry. *I understand it was in your area of expertise....*"

—*Submitted by:* Lyn Donovan, R.D.H.
Cerritos, CA

"SURGERY....FOR A BRIDE"

*A*n eighteen year old airman reported to the dental clinic with a lacerated lingual frenum (the thread-like cord of muscle under the tongue, which attaches it to the floor of the mouth). Upon examination by the attending dentist, it was noted that the laceration lined up, perfectly, with the incisal edges of the lower mandibular incisors (front teeth) when the tongue was fully protruded.

"Airman Likor, when did you first notice or experience this problem?" Captain Nelson asked the concerned young patient.

"Actually, that's what I can't understand. It seems to come and go. Like it always seems worse on Sunday nights. I don't know, Sir."

Captain Nelson, having been in the Air Force Dental Corp. for 15 months, was certainly not the most experienced dentist in the clinic. He did, however, finish #1 in his dental class and had already been described as "unusually gifted and insightful," by his commanding officer.

"Uh, Mr. Likor do you perhaps have a girlfriend?"

"Yes, sir, I sure do, Captain! As a matter of fact, I've really been pushing her to marry me, *but so far she won't say yes.*"

"Do you see her during the week, or just on the weekends?" Nelson asked, as he tried, delicately as possible, to determine why the injury seemed to recur on the weekends, particularly noticed by the young airman on Sunday nights.

After more questions were put to the patient, centered around his relationship with his hoped-for bride, he finally caught on and both the dentist and his patient had a great laugh. Two weeks later, the young airman came back to clinic and asked if an operation could be performed which would prevent, or, at least, reduce the chances for re-injury to the area....

As things sometimes happen, Dr. Nelson had just returned from a staff meeting where the topic of discussion had been concern for why the dental residents had not been receiving enough surgical experiences, or case work. Nelson, never slow on the uptake, saw an opportunity to "kill two birds with one stone." He immediately referred the patient to the residency clinic for a lingual frenectomy (essentially, the removal of the muscle which **limits** the tongue's forward movement).

The surgery apparently achieved a good result, since Nelson received a wedding invitation three months later, along with the following note from the bride-to-be....

"Doctor, the operation on Louis was *a wonderful success.* Thank you so much for a job well done!!!"

—*Submitted by:* William T. Neely, III, D.M.D.
Plattsburgh, N.Y.

"DENTAL, EVANGELICAL, OR CHICKEN BONES.....?"

*R*on McCollor, another Arizona dentist who preaches and practices the theory that humor is the only way to live and work, retired from practice at the ripe old age of 55. I'm positive his attitude that "dentistry was more like a hobby I loved doing," was one reason he might have pulled off early retirement. Anyway, this guy cracked me up with a tape he made in response to my letter of solicitation seeking humorous episodes. So, here's Ron....

Patient came in with a severe toothache. Dr. McCollor confirmed his clinical exam with x-rays:

"Sorry, Mr. Obtusca, but the decay is so deep that the tooth will have to be removed, or have a root canal done," Ron said, as he held the film up and studied it again in the patient's presence.

"Doc, I don't want it pulled."

"Good! We'll do a root canal....."

"No, sir, I definitely don't want one of them things.

I've heard about how much they cost, and hurt. Nope, I ain't having no root canals done! What's another option?"

Ron, having gone through this scenario a hundred times before with similar patient types, decided it was time to offer his third option.....

"Well," he said, with his hand placed gently on the patient's shoulder, "we could use our *evangelical approach....*"

"Meaning what?" the patient asked, with an askance glance, first at Ron, then at the assistant.

"Oh, I mean we could say.... 'Tooth, Be Healed In The Name Of The Lord!!!!'"

"Hell, Doc, I'm serious. Ain't there nothing else besides pulling it or doing a root canal?"

Ron, now knowing, beyond a shadow of a doubt, he was dealing with the type of patient who's looking for an instant panacea....at little or no cost or pain.....responded with a fourth option.

"Actually, while working out there on the Indian reservation, I did learn some pretty interesting dental treatment from one of the fellows out there...."

"What's that, Doc?" the patient impatiently inter-rupted.

"Well, we could form a circle in the sand, throw some chicken bones in there, and beat on a drum, and it might go away."

Before the patient could respond, Irma, his assis-tant and witness to many similar office scenarios, piped up, **"I'm not putting on those feathers anymore today, and jumping in and out of that circle, beating on that drum!!!"**

The patient, now sure he was in the office of two certified nutcases said, **"Oh, heck, Doc, just take the darn thing out. I'm getting tired just thinking about all these options you've got!"**

—*Submitted by:* Ronald S. McCollor, D.D.S.
Sun City West, AZ

"PROPER CHOICE OF WORDS....?"

*L*yn Donovan, a registered hygienist in the offices of Drs. Philip R. Jen Kin and Robert M. Miyasaki, graduated from dental hygiene school in Canada. The following story confirms a simple word, though usually not as professionally acceptable, might be safer to use when giving patient instructions than one which more properly conveys a dental education. Sometimes, the latter can be difficult for the patient comprehension whereas, at other times, the professional might find it trouble for the tongue.....

From my comprehension of the report, the hygiene school in Canada, like so many of the earlier professional schools of dentistry and hygiene, had the older type dental units. This also holds true for the first schools in the United States. Probably all over the world, for that matter. Those units, unlike the state-of-the-art equipment seen in many of today's dental schools, had individual cuspidor bowls attached to them.

Even though the great number of patients appreciated being able to lean over and empty their mouth of saliva and debris, modern day studies confirmed the loss of time and efficiency each time a patient was given the opportunity to perform this little ritual. So, for better or worse, the units are now mostly devoid of the old cuspidor bowl. However, with the units in Lyn's Canadian hygiene school still having them, she and her fellow students were constantly being admonished not to use the word *spit*, when telling a patient to empty their mouth. Their instructors instructed and continually reinforced the word, **expectorate**, should be used in place of *spit*.

One of Lyn's classmates, a girl who might have been having a bad day or, in the moment of experiencing a Freudian slip, had trouble with the chosen word one day. A day which forever changed the course of this lady's own career, verbally, thereafter. She also provided sidesplitting, rolling on the floor type of laughter for Lyn and the other hygienists within earshot of her and the patient in her unit on that fateful day.

At the moment when the young hygienist recognized her patient's mouth was about as full as he could stand it, with saliva and pumice debris, she stopped and, very professionally, told him....

"Okay, you may now sit up and *ejaculate*!"

Aftermath: According to Lyn, this hygienist never attempted to use the word expectorate again, no matter what was said to her by the instructors. She also, to Lyn and other classmate's knowledge, has never attempted use of the word again in her entire hygienist career. The episode, besides the moment of hysterical humor it provided for Lyn at the time, still provides the food for a good laugh anytime she hears the word expectorate used, instead of *spit*.....

—*Submitted by:* Lyn Donovan, R.D.H.
Cerritos, CA

"SOY BOBITA...."

*T*his story was submitted to me by a practicing attorney, a man who also holds a degree in dentistry. An exceptional and rare bird, indeed. He practiced oral and maxillofacial surgery for 15 years before entering law school. As I understand, his dental practice was located in the "upper ghetto" of New York City, the birthplace of stories which have evolved into true gems. I'm not sure if the locale of his office drove him to seek a career in law, out of survival, or if he is simply one of those guys with an insatiable appetite for the challenge and reward which comes from high scholastic endeavor and achievement.

What I do know about Alan M. Novich, D.D.S., JD, with historical certainty, is his lifetime possession and use of a profound comedic sense. The best evidence, documenting this observation and statement, comes from a former classmate of his at Loyola-Chicago, Dr. Ted Kiersch of Tucson, Arizona. Besides his reputation as the court jester, of sorts, Dr. Kiersch and others have recognized Alan's ability to couch his thoughts in a writing style which is clear and entertaining. He is no dilettante in expressing himself with the written word! I don't know Alan, personally, but his sense of humor certainly came across in the first letter I ever received from him.

Alan's first story involved a long-time surgical assistant of his, Barbara (called Bobbi by the office staff), and a Spanish patient who was in the office for an oral surgical procedure. As was the usual custom of Dr. Novich, the procedure was initiated by first trying to insure the patient was completely relaxed, prior to beginning sedation. During the course of his attempt to relax the Spanish girl, the following exchange took place.

"Como se llama, usted?" Alan asked. ("What is your name?")

"Soy Hermasita," she replied. ("I am Hermasita.")

Dr. Novich smiled at her and said, "Soy Alanita." ("I am Alan.")

Alan's greeting in the patient's native tongue was now followed with nurse #1 saying "Soy Vikita." The patient grinned.

Nurse #2, being no dummy and seeing the patient's

grin begin to grow into a smile which was now showing teeth and the obvious signs of comfort and relaxation with the staff, jumped in with, "Soy Peggita!"

As all in the room now turned their attention and full focus upon the only staff member left to introduce herself, Bobbi shouted out, "Soy Bobita!"

The patient's big smile suddenly turned into an almost uncontrollable laughter with Bobbi's self introduction. Besides the patient, Dr. Novich was the only person in the room who immediately understood the spanish significance. "Soy Bobita," unbeknownst to Bobbi, means **"I am a dummy!"** The patient was now so relaxed the i.v. solution was a snap!

—*Submitted by:* Alan M. Novich, Attorney at Law
New York, NY

"ONE FOR TWO"

*D*r. David V. Haning had been in practice only two years when the following event took place....

David, like so many of the young dentists mentioned in the stories, was intensely devoted to pleasing patients with his work. He took great pride, as I'm sure he still does, in doing the best possible dentistry on each patient treated. He was especially dedicated to making exceptional dentures, one reason for this being the greater demand for this dental skill in the area where he had located.

So, as the story was related to me, young Dr. Haning made a lower denture for a 75 year old coal miner. Upon placement of the completed denture, the smiling miner was told to please return to the office on Monday to have the post insertion evaluation David always liked to do. Normally, he did the denture examination within 24 hours of its initial placement, but being it was a Friday afternoon, the miner was told to return on the upcoming Monday.

Monday came and went, as the saying goes, and only when David was closing the office front door, did he realize the old miner had not returned for his denture checkup. Inwardly, David Haning worried over it the rest of the evening. He knew the 75 year old patient did not have a phone, and he was hoping the old guy hadn't developed some severe sore spots, then simply took the denture out, never to put them in again except to go to church or for some other social encounter.

Many denture stories are in circulation, confirming the potential realities for Dr. Haning's concerns, and he didn't want his denture to be yet another negative statistic. Part of his fretting, quite naturally, was the pride he had in his work. But, for the most part, his concern was due to the genuine affection he had for the miner. He really liked him, and he wanted him to enjoy the denture he had made....

Several weeks came and went, with no sign signalling the return of David's lower denture patient. Some of the old man's relatives came in, but no one seemed to know much about how the miner and his wife were faring, certainly not in reference to the recently made denture. These mountain folks didn't share a lot of their health history with others, so it was no real surprise to David that no one seemed to know much.

Finally, after almost a month, the old man suddenly appeared at the waiting room window. David's assistant quickly gave him the news of the old miner being in the office....

"Good morning, Mr. Bronson! Where in the world have you been?"

The old patient informed David, quite pleasantly, how he'd been occupied with work around the home place and just hadn't found the time to get back in until now.

"Oh, I understand," David said, "but I want to know how in the heck that denture is doing?"

The patient responded he really loved his dentures, hadn't experienced the first sore spot and, even better yet, his wife also loved his dentures....

David's pride, as he tells me, had just started to swell from all the praise given by the miner, when he noticed the patient did not have the denture in his mouth.

"Mr. Bronson, I thought you said you loved the denture, but I don't see you wearing it. Do you have a sore spot I need to relieve?"

The old man answered David's question with a toothless smile by saying:

"Why, heck no, Doc David, I ain't got no sore spot a tal. I tol ye that my wif luved the plate bout as good as me. Matter of fact, she luvs the darn thang so much, she's a'warin it bout haf the time. Rite now, she's got that thar plate in her own mouf and I'm a'havin to gum it today, Doc."

Postscript: The denture was obviously so pleasing to Mr. Bronsen and his spouse, poor David never did get to make a denture for the man's wife.....

—*Submitted by:* David V. Haning, D.M.D.
Shinniston, WV

"FIRST, THEY GOTTA HAVE THE BASICS..."

*S*ix year old little Johnny's mother brought him to the dental office of Dr. William Kates, after being up all night with a toothache. Unfortunately, it was his very first visit to a dental office. Dr. Kates took an x-ray and determined there was a large abscess causing the pain. He advised little Johnny the tooth had to come out and it would be as painless as he could possibly make the procedure.

Gingerly, Bill Kates administered the local anesthetic (the shot) and, quite to his amazement, the little guy didn't whimper the first word of protest. Bill proceeded, though cautiously, with the actual removal of the tooth. Again, to his astonishment, the boy didn't make the first sound, not even a grimace.

With the bad tooth now satisfactorily extracted on a child who had made his first visit appear to be old hat, Dr. Kates began to profusely praise the boy's behavior and, in fact, told him to take a toy home from the office "treasure chest."

Bill, like most dentists, also showed the boy the tooth that had caused him so much pain the night before, and told him to take it home, place it under his pillow, and the "tooth fairy" would surely leave some money for such a "big boy..."

Kates then turned his back to little Johnny and began to make entry notes in his dental record. Suddenly, and totally unexpected, he heard loud crying and sobbing from the boy. He immediately turned to see the child shedding alligator tears.....

"Johnny, what can possibly be the matter? That old tooth is gone and we don't have to do anything else at all," Bill Kates quickly comforted, thinking that perhaps the boy was either letting go of some stored anxiety, after the fact, or the tooth extraction had actually hurt more than the boy let on to him.

The boy's response to Dr. Kate's question, between sobs, was.....

"The tooth fairy can't come see me...." he answered, with more tears and crying.

"Why in the world would the tooth fairy not come to see a boy as big and strong as you've been this morning....?"

"Cause I don't sleep with a *pillow*!!"

Dental Moral: We dentists had better make sure "our kids" have the basic implements needed for our old colleague, the tooth fairy, to leave her monetary reward, before we make promises...Huh?

—*Submitted by:* **William Kates, D.D.S.**
Pasadena, CA

"THE GREAT PHOENIX BRUSHFIRE...."

K en Snyder, an Arizona dentist who truly understands and appreciates the value of humor, presents workshops on the subject. He clearly comprehends the indispensable ingredient its role is in realizing a successful over-all practice, the essential nature of nurturing the trait in employees and, for his own health. Ken's story shows how humor was used to defuse a potential management problem.

Dr. Snyder had just hired a new dental assistant and, being it was her first day on the job, she was anxious to please everyone, particularly him. In Ken's words, "she was very bright and attentive." One of the afternoon appointments was a patient scheduled for root canal therapy, and Snyder had high hopes and confidence the new assistant would handle her duties with ease and expertise.

Just as he thought, the procedure went without a hitch. The new assistant did her tasks with admirable aplomb. After the procedure was completed, she also demonstrated her organizational skills while putting away the supplies and placing instruments into sterilization. One piece of equipment she put away was an alcohol torch, which Ken used to warm his instruments before sealing the root canal's gutta percha. It uses denatured alcohol to provide a clear, smoke-free flame. The assistant had neatly placed this in one of the laboratory's cabinets, underneath a shelf containing boxes of cellophane wrapped toothbrushes.

Twenty minutes later, the smell of smoke had Dr. Snyder, Mary, his receptionist, Linda, his hygienist, and the new assistant all running around the office trying to sniff out the source. They all arrived in the lab, at about the same moment, their olfactory senses accurately leading them to the visual sight of smoke snaking itself from underneath the cabinet where the new assistant had placed the burner.

The fire was quickly extinguished with an extinguisher with the only casualties being the toothbrushes and the new assistant's pride. Dr. Ken Snyder knew he was about to face a management crisis as the new employee sheepishly asked.... "Dr. Snyder, am I going to be fired?" Knowing every eye was on him, and each pair of ears keenly tuned for his response, he realized his words would have to be carefully chosen. But, before he could answer, his receptionist answered with....

"Why, heck no! This is going to make our office famous."

"Say what?" came the unanimous response, as all heads turned towards Mary.

"Sure, we'll call the press, the TV stations, the camera crews....do you all realize this is the first time, ever, for a **brushfire in a dental office?"**

Everyone broke out in laughter and work was resumed....with peace of mind for the new dental assistant and, with Ken Snyder's realization that his living the philosophy of "always try to find humor in a situation" had obviously rubbed off on his employees.

—Submitted by: **Ken Snyder, D.D.S.**
Phoenix, AZ

"THE SMITHSONIAN SAMPLES"

*F*orensic dentistry has created a comparatively new area of interest and expertise in the field. The work itself, which is identification of the deceased and sometimes decomposed remains of human beings, is actually not new at all. In the past, it was done by general dentists using their x-rays and clinical treatment records to identify the oftentimes mutilated or deteriorated remains.

Today, there seems to be a growing number of dentists who enjoy prominence in the area of forensics. Some have advanced training in oral pathology or other areas, whereas, many are still general dentists who have limited their practices to this field of practice.

This story comes from the northwestern United States, from the area where a recent serial killer was born and did much of his killing. I think the fact that Dr. John Mooreland, the dentist who submitted the story, practices in the state of Washington and is involved with forensics, may be one reason my imaginative interest was stimulated when I received his letter. After getting into the meat of the report, not to make an obscene pun, I quickly discerned this was going to be anything except high drama......

It seems a body had been found in a deep ravine, the victim of a motorcycle accident several months prior to the discovery. The county coroner had worked with John Mooreland and his associate on other cases, and therefore immediately solicited Mooreland's assistance.

There had been considerable soft tissue decomposition, but there was still some remaining skin and scalp on the skull. It was not a pretty sight, certainly not the type of face one would like to see on a guy your daughter brings home for Thanksgiving dinner.

The coroner requested dental x-rays and the victim's head was thereby sent to Dr. Mooreland's office in a cardboard box. I cannot attest to this being the usual conveyance container for evidential remains of this sort! Apparently, it caused no breach in the forensic routine, since Mooreland proceeded with his work upon receiving the remains.

Now, at the time Dr. John was doing his work-up on the skull, his partner was collecting some urine samples from his staff in order to do a mercury screening analysis....the now somewhat lukewarm issue on how much mercury in silver fillings is being absorbed into patient's tissues. Anyway, the urine samples were put in a box, and placed in the general lab, for pickup by the medical lab the office used for this service.

The next day the box of urine samples was picked up by the medical lab courier. Approximately 30 minutes later, the office of Dr. Mooreland received a phone call from a rather distraught medical lab technician. The following conversation insued between Jane, the receptionist for Dr. Mooreland and his partner, and the lab. (I do confess the dialogue conveys some imaginative insights on my part.)

"Janie, this is Becky, down at the lab...."

"Oh, hi, Bec, thought you guys just left here."

"We did, dear, but I've got a slight problem over here....listen, is Dr. Mooreland around?"

"Well, yes, he is Becky, but I think he's in the lab doing some pretty high priority stuff for the coroners office. I really hate to bug him, you know. Can I help you with the problem?"

"Yeah, I guess so. Listen, you need to ask those guys

out there what type of samples are in the box Roger just picked up. He was green when he came in here, really bitching about his car stinking to high heaven and how someone was going to have to pay for cleaning it out. I'm telling you, he was going off like crazy...Now, I know why!"

"Why?" Jane asked, with obvious puzzlement in her voice.

"Janie, I was really tied up when he came in and I admit I just passed his mouth off to him being like he is....you know Rog. So, I told him to set the box down and go take a hike for a while. Anyway, after a few minutes the lab was ruined. No one in here will go near enough to the box to give me the samples."

"I don't understand, Bec, those were the urine samples for mercury analysis. They were fairly fresh, as far as I know....I can't imagine."

"If those are urine samples, Janie baby, they've been taken from the Smithsonian museum. I'm telling you, this stuff is rank."

Jane, even though she was office receptionist for both doctors, had just returned from vacation this morning and was therefore unaware of the present forensic case being worked on by Dr. Mooreland.

"Becky, hold on, let me see if he can come to the phone. I really don't know what to tell you."

"Right, Jane, why don't you do that.. I know those two sometimes do some weird stuff out there and I want to be real sure before one of my people puts their hands into something that is hazardous...."

Just about the time the chief lab technician had "hazardous" out of her mouth, a blood curdling scream took place about 15 feet behind her. Becky jumped a good six inches off the floor, dropped the phone, and spun around to see Elizabeth Hansen, a petite technician with two months experience who had just come on duty for the day, bent over the opened cardboard box....her right and left hands cupped over each of her eyes, as she screamed out:

"It's a body!!!! Somebody's been murdered....." and headed for the lab's exit, one hand covering her mouth and the other holding her stomach as she ran, bent over, through the double door......

—*Submitted by:* **John Mooreland, D.D.S.**
Port Orchard, WA

"AUNT BEA'S GOLD TOOTH...."

*O*f all the dental stories I've received from colleagues across the country, I'd have to say this is one of my favorites. Maybe because it touched a warped part of my brain? I'm not sure. But, I do know I chuckled for hours after reading it. I'm even smiling right now, as I write these words! Perhaps it was the Elmer Gantry thing, and the blind faith followers of those kind of guys that got me. Maybe it was because I remember, vividly, how many crazy things seemed to happen to me when I was the age of this dentist when he had his "Aunt Bea" experience. It's hard to say. However, I can see, with my mind's eye, the face of Dr. Reinhardt Tillitzky and his assistant when they encountered this sweet "Lulu" of a lady....

Reinhardt was fresh out of the University of Florida College of Dentistry and, like I was in the summer of '69, excited about greeting a new patient, *actually any patient for that matter.*

During his very first weeks of practice, one of the new patients on his book was an elderly lady who had phoned in for an appointment to have her teeth cleaned and a certain tooth checked for "color changes." On the day she arrived at the office for her initial visit, Dr. Tillitzky remembers his first impression of her was the remarkable resemblance she had to Aunt Bea on the then popular Andy Griffith show. She came in wearing a bright summer dress, with matching purse, and was so warm and bubbly that Reinhardt was simply thrilled to have her as one of his very first patients.

Upon doing the clinical examination of her teeth, he found nothing of real significance. She had great oral hygiene and no complaint per se, however, as he was about to compliment her on the excellent home-care she'd obviously been maintaining, she sat up in the chair, looked at him with a seriously, earnest look, and asked:

"Doctor Reinhardt, do you see any color changes in my lower left molar?"

Reinhardt, placing his mirror back in the patient's mouth, and studying the area very carefully, responded with, "No, Ma'am, I certainly don't. Is the tooth hurting you in some way?" he asked, as he now recalled she had listed the molar as an area of concern on the "chief complaint" part of her health-history questionnaire. Reinhardt immediately felt a little awkward and remiss for not addressing her concern before she reminded him.

"Oh, for heaven's sake, no. But you know, Doctor, my former dentist told me the tooth would need to be crowned someday and that really started to worry me, and all."

"I can understand you might have been somewhat alarmed to hear that," Reinhardt said, "but I really can't see the need for worrying about it. As a matter of fact, I think the tooth looks pretty good, myself."

"Well, you know what, Doctor, it actually started bothering me so much that when we all went out to the revival meeting last Sunday night, I asked the preacher to please pray for my tooth. And, that's exactly what he did! In fact, the preacher laid his hands on my cheeks and *asked God to grant me a gold tooth*....are you sure there are no changes in it, Dr. Tillitzky?"

Because Reinhardt couldn't stand the thought of

hurting "Aunt Bea's" feelings, he studied the tooth again with his patient examining mirror, and replied, "Ma'am, *now that I've looked at it again, it does seem to be turning a little yellow.* Now, isn't that interesting?" he said, while glancing over at his assistant.

Tillitzky's assistant rolled her eyes to the ceiling, as he continued with, "You know, I think we'll just keep an eye on it."

"Are you sure there's no gold yet, Doctor?" she asked in a pleading tone.

"Well, not yet, *but we should give it a little more time,*" he responded.

With the appointment completed, Reinhardts's assistant escorted the somewhat disappointed lady out to the front office. As "Aunt Bea" was saying goodbye, she made the following parting statement:

"Oh, dear, I'm so glad I came to Dr. Reinhardt. He's such a wonderful man and his saying the tooth looked like it was *turning slightly yellow* has just made my day. **I know it won't be long now before the preacher's prayer for a gold tooth is going to come to pass....!**"

—*Submitted by:* Reinhardt H. Tillitzky, D.M.D.
Barberville, FL

"The Commander in Chief...."

*H*ere is another California story....one that is hysterically humorous, in the aftermath and after-thoughts of some heart pounding moments for several individuals in the dental office of Barbara and Robert J. Porporato.

Things were going smoothly on that fateful morning, according to Barbara, the receptionist and office manager, until 10:45 a.m. At that time, one of Dr. Porporato's older patients, Mrs. Rose, arrived at the office 15 minutes ahead of her 11 a.m appointment. As Barbara later learned, the sweet little lady had gone by the bank and withdrawn $300 before coming to the office. She had simply arrived at the dental office earlier than she anticipated.

Barbara, being the receptionist and the loving wife of Dr. Porporato, had those certain inalienable and vested rights of interest in the practice which made it a cinch for the elderly patient to feel perfectly comfortable and at home. She didn't bother reminding her she was early, knowing this was the general habit of other senior patients in their practice. It wouldn't surprise me if she silently thought how nice it would be if some of their younger patients, those who were chronically late for appointments, could develop this habit of the more mature patients.

Anyway, Mrs. Rose had seated herself in the chair closest to the reception room entrance door. Perhaps because it had a very comfortable cushion in it. Perhaps she was simply tired from going by the bank first, and therefore sat in the chair closest to where she entered. I'm not sure. I do know the patient was elderly; in her mid- 70s; had just withdrawn $300 dollars in cash from the bank; was 15 minutes early for her appointment; and had her right arm through the double straps of a large black purse. She, like many ladies who have come to the practice, held the purse with a secure arm lock.

The next thing to unfold in the evolving drama was the entrance into the reception room of a man whom Barbara intuitively knew did not belong in their office.

She was on the phone at the time he entered and made his initial eye contact with her. He understood she recognized, instantly, he was out of place, and she knew, in the same awareness and perception, he had received the visual transmission of her analysis....as he quickly turned, mumbling something under his breath, and left the office. Not one word had been exchanged between the man and our astute receptionist, but the reflection in her eyes of his being so totally out of sync was obviously enough to make him vacate the premises.

On the side of unfortunate things in this world, one has to acknowledge that the criminal element has taken to heart and head....maybe to a greater degree than the more non-sociopathic types....the fact that the patience and persistence usually pays off for them. Certainly in the short run of their malovent intentions. After a matter of seconds, our party pooper was back at the dental gala. This time he excused his body from the main room, choosing rather to thrust his arm through a door cracked only wide enough to allow an arm appendage of his doubtful humanity into the sanctum of Barbara and Robert J. Porporato's dental office. It came through that tiny opening like the head of some insidious reptile, striking with premeditation and swift silence!

"Stop, thief!!!" the little old lady cried loud enough to make a veteran NFL quarterback on Super Bowl day appear to have a bad case of laryngitis.

Barbara, not being slow in the uptake of what had just happened, immediately ordered her 50-year-old husband-dentist into action with, **"Robert, go after that guy!! He just snatched your patient's purse!"** Right behind her impeccably clear instructions to Dr. Robert J., she phoned 911 and gave them the report.

Now, if one were to think Barbara Porporato, diligent receptionist and dedicated spouse, was through with her orders, then one would be seriously in error. The next high command fell on the ears of the 30 year old male patient still seated in Dr. Porporato's dental chair, as she shouted new instructions, **"Look out that window, and don't you dare take your eyes off that running thief!!!"**

Our receptionist then turned her attention to the victim, emotionally traumatized, but fortunately, not physically injured. She gently calmed Mrs. Rose, but instructions were still issuing forth from the mouth of our vigilant receptionist as she prompted the little old gal to please recall the physical features and details of her assailant....with particular emphasis for her to try and clearly describe that snake-like arm that struck and snatched.

Meanwhile, Dr. Porporato, all 50 years of muscle, bone and spirit, was running lickity split down the rear stairs of the medical-dental building, then, down the side street taken by the fleeing feet of the purse snatcher. As our heroic dentist later reflected, he thought his youthful, male patient was right behind him during the chase. Of course not, remember, our **commander in chief**, Barbara, had ordered him to track the thief...but, only with his eyes!

Now, to make matters worse, when the good dentist returned to his office after giving up the chase, he learned, with some sense of sad realism, I'm sure, his wife had been on the phone with their insurance agent (isn't it absolutely mind boggling, how much she had accomplished in a matter of minutes) and the insurance guy had supposedly closed the conversation with, *"Barb, if the suspect shoots 'Ol Bob', you're going to be one rich gal, my dear....!"*

Can you imagine, really, the sobering thoughts Bob Porporato, D.D.S., must have had following the insurance agent's words to his wife. I mean, here is a guy who was minding his own business, *simply grinning and grinding,* in his own little dental world.....waiting on his next patient, when all this serious stuff begins to erupt. Then, at the orders of his devoted spouse and receptionist, out of his office he goes....gloved, masked, lab coat and feet flying after a man he doesn't know jack shit about! The police later told him the man was in his early twenties, quite muscular and from the looks of him, certainly capable of causing great bodily harm to a 50'ish dentist type. Can you imagine Robert's heart rate when he received that piece of information?

I can't say what California or Daly City has done or offered to do, but I do feel, in all sincerity, this is a **true American hero**. Don't you? Surely this man deserves, if not state or local recognition, then at least the attention some of the Boy Scouts of America receive for similar feats of heroism. And, what about the quick thinking and fast acting spouse and receptionist, Barbara? Doesn't she deserve some formal tribute....or, promotion? **Maybe that fifth star....?**

—*Submitted by:* Robert J. Porporato, D.D.S
and Barbara Porporato, wife-receptionist
Daly City, CA

"A MATTER OF SEMANTICS...."

*D*r. J.E. Pewitt, being fresh out of dental school and recently set up in his own private practice was, like so many dentists at the unique stage in their careers, extremely focused on his endeavor to please each new patient he treated. Of the utmost importance in building a private practice is the creation of a reputation for causing little to no pain when giving the shot of local anesthetic. Dr. Pewitt had, in his own approach to insuring this realization for his patients, found certain vocalizations could create mental analogies that were calming and useful in obtaining this end. He used terms like "a little pinch," "a tug on your cheek," "a mosquito bite" and a number of others. They all seemed to be effective.

One afternoon, when preparing to give an injection to an exceptionally pretty young lady, Dr. Pewitt became fiercely focused on "being extra good" with the needle. After all, he was not married at the time and knew that one never knows what might develop, if one is successful at imprinting an indelible impression of gentleness on the opposite sex, particularly with a needle in one's hand.

Just as he started to insert the needle's tip into the

patient's tissue, he said, with the words warm and smooth enough to melt butter, "Okay, now you're going to feel something *like a little prick* **under your lip....**"

"Prick" had just cleared his mouth when he paused, instantly focusing his eyes dead into hers....the laughter, from both of them, erupted with a spontaneity that confirmed this was an analogy Doc Pewitt would have to watch in the future.... **"a rose, by any other name...."** **not applicable in this case!**

—*Submitted by:* Dr. J.E. Pewitt
Gulf Breeze, FL

"PERSEVERANCE AND PASSING...."

*T*he dental school education, as described in some of the other stories, fosters idealism, while, at the same time, creating some not so ideal patient experiences. A potential explanation is the necessary evil of imposing number requirements, to be completed for each of every dental procedure a future dentist is expected to encounter, before the student is qualified for graduation. This story is another one of those student-patient encounters, where striving for idealism and the perseverance to get those rigid requirements fulfilled, came face to face.....a not so ideal situation.

The patient was a 74 year old Italian immigrant, his speech still thick with accent, who had come to the dental school seeking a new pair of upper and lower dentures. It would be his fifth or sixth pair. None had been satisfactory! The student was in his fourth year and exactly one complete denture requirement short of graduation....one of those less than ideal unions.

From the very start, it was clearly evident the patient would be hard to manage. He was hyperactive, even at his mature age, but whenever the student would ask him to try and relax, the old fellow would remind the young dentist that he was still a young man. In fact, he would brag on "still being a rooster with the women." This, in spite of his actual age and the fact that he lived with his 96-year-old father.

None of this detoured the faithful student from his objective....that last pair of dentures he needed to graduate, not even the fact that the patient would bring his "bag full of previous dentures" each time he had an appointment at the school. Always, he would "instruct" the student on "how to correctly do the particular procedure" being carried out at that appointment. The persevering student simply laughed at the old man's statements, hoping whatever he was saying with that thick accent was a joke.

Finally, some several months later, the dentures were completed. They were beautiful and the student was proud of his achievement. That should have been it....graduation credit for the student and a content patient. Alas, the patient was unhappy with yet another set of dentures. Each time he would attempt to convey the reason for his discontent, he would spit the lower denture out and catch it in mid air. It was, in the student's mind, his attempt to show the lower had no retention, yet, when the faculty would check the retention, they would find it was actually better than average.

As graduation day neared, the dentures were still not checked off. Things looked bleak indeed. The faculty could not change the rules held to for decades, and the patient was not going to pretend to be happy when he was not. In desperation, the student decided to do a reline of the new dentures, hoping that it might solve some unseen problem. The faculty gave permission to get on with the reline attempt.

If the dentures had been a failure, the reline was disastrous. At the moment of loading each denture with the impression material, to take up any space or voids, the student overloaded both. In moments, the gooey, rubbery, stinking stuff was flowing out of the patient's mouth, down his chin and onto the arms of the student. In a few more moments, the patient began to gag and choke, his face turning blood red as he strained to get air through chronically inflamed and congested nasal passages. The gagging was very shortly followed by the patient's breakfast and lunch being served to the student....it was running down his arms and dripping off his elbows.

Still the intrepid student persevered and hung on for the final seconds needed to allow setting of the material.

The dentures were pulled from the mouth and, upon inspection, indicated there had been a terrible reline! The patient recovered, quite rapidly, and acted like what had just taken place was a normal part of his every day life. The student, literally covered with the unpleasant sight, and smell of food eaten hours earlier, and a sorry looking denture reline in his wet and clammy hands, was almost too embarrassed to call one of the professors over to check the completed procedure off for a grade. Finally, desperation to get that graduation credit over-ruled his fear and shame....the grade, as written on the denture grade card..... **"Passed By Perseverance."**

—*Submitted by:* **Bruce G. Knecht, D.M.D.**
Coconut Creek, FL

"A SUDDEN DEMOTION...."

My present hygienist, Josie Dye, had just moved to New Orleans back in the mid '70s and, being without a license to practice as a hygienist in Louisiana, she took an interim position of dental assistant in the office of Dr. John Shea. As good fortune sometimes falls, Josie's new dentist, besides being recognized as one of the area's prominent crown and fixed bridge practitioners, was also a member of the Louisiana State Board of Dental Examiners....the agency that grants licenses to dentists and hygienists.

Naturally, Josie soon received a temporary license to practice dental hygiene in Louisiana, but, when called upon, continued to assist Dr. Shea at the chair when not doing her hygiene work. One morning she was scheduled to see a five year old girl and, before actually starting the cleaning procedure, Josie took the time to introduce herself and briefly explain what she was about to do.....

"Good morning, Debbie, I'm Josie, the *hygienist.* I'm going to clean your teeth so they'll be real pretty for your first day at kindergarten. When I finish, I'll go get Dr. Shea so he can check your teeth for any cavities. Okay?"

The little girl, timid and afraid as kids this age usually are in a dental office, nodded her approval and Josie thus proceeded with the cleaning. The child was great, not whimpering the first time. When Josie finished, she advised the little girl she was now going to momentarily leave the room so she could go and get Dr. Shea.

Shea, a man well-known for his beautiful gold inlays and crown work, was also highly respected for his dedicated work on the state board. In a word, he was renown for his dentistry and contributions to the profession in many other ways. He was accustomed, though not big-headed, to the elevated status he enjoyed in the dental community.

"Debbie, this is Dr. Shea. He's going to now check your teeth," Josie said, as she introduced the little girl to the dentist.

"Hello, Debbie. Josie's told me you have some really nice teeth. You don't mind if I take a look do you?" Shea cautiously asked, knowing the importance of maintaining the confidence and rapport that Josie had now established.

"Hello," the little girl timidly responded. "You must be the *low dentist*."

"The what dentist?" Shea asked, thinking he didn't correctly hear what she had said.

"The *low dentist*," the little girl said, this time with a little more animation in her voice.

"Why do you say, *low dentist*, sweetheart?" John Shea curiously inquired, realizing that he was a little over six feet tall.

"Cause Josie's already told me she's the "*high-dentist*".....so you must be the low dentist....!"

—*Submitted by:* **Josie Dye, R.D.H.**
Jackson, MS

"So, where's the shotgun....?"

*I*t's one thing to be embarrassed, another to be humiliated! The former is like a slap on the cheek. It stings. It causes self-consciousness. The other is like a kick in the groin. It is agonizing. One becomes mortified with the pain....

This story, submitted by Harold Schachter, D.D.S., M.S., an orthodontist in Ocean, New Jersey, provides a crystal clear example of public humiliation. It has all the criteria necessary to meet the word's meaning....There was the public crucifixion. The shame. The pernicious pain. The discomfort, even when read about, is painfully palpable. It's like one can literally feel the terrible entry of those fangs which pierced the victim....real, or imagined!

You thought this was a book of dental humor? How could humiliation possibly be humorous, you ask? Remember, I previously asserted the nature of that tenuous thread between anxiety, pain and humor. That same boundary separates deep humiliation, shame, from humor which becomes hysterical when, thank God, the relief valve of laughter is finally able to be opened.

Harold Schachter, like many orthodontists who do exceptionally fine work, has enjoyed a successful practice. His, located in the Jersey Shore area, had blossomed to a full bloom about the time this incident happened. His practice did not fortuitously flower, but was due, in large part, to the hundreds of smiling teenagers and young adults he cosmetically improved through the specialty of orthodontics.

Harold is good, and it has paid off with the dividends of referrals, particularly referrals from satisfied families. It is not unusual for Dr. Schachter to treat two or three siblings from the same family, perhaps over a period of time spanning 10 years between the time the oldest child is treated and, when the youngest one receives his or her orthodontic care.

One Thursday afternoon, according to Schachter, the treatment area was filled with the after school crowd of kids. The waiting room was also packed, jammed with the familiar faces of parents and patients waiting on their child to complete treatment for the day or, to be seen. Also, among the faces in the waiting room, were the young toddlers that moms had brought along to wait on older brother or sister. It was always like this in Harold's waiting room. One reason being, other than his own great reputation, his associate, Dr. Lang. One good orthodontist is usually busy, two, and you have something like a McDonald's at rush hour.

On this particular afternoon, Dr. Schachter had just completed the day's treatment on a pre-teen youngster, a young boy whose older sister, Nancy, had received ortho treatment from him several years ago. The boy's mother was waiting on him in the reception room and Dr. Schachter, being the kind of dentist who likes to regularly touch base with his patient's parents, in person, decided to walk out with young Bobby and speak to his mother, Mrs. Smith.

Casually walking into the room with the boy, Harold exchanged warm greetings with Mrs. Smith as she stood up to meet him and Bobby. He began telling the mother about her son's orthodontic progress and openly praised the boy's cooperation with the treatment thus far. Praises which were legitimately deserved. This pre- teen youth was one of those kids who not only made treatment a cinch, he was one of those rare ones who kept his teeth immaculately clean. His home-care, alone, was worth the applause being given by his orthodontist.

During the course of their conversation, Mrs. Smith began to discuss her older daughter, Nancy, attempting, as Harold now sees with the clarity of 20-20 hindsight, to convey her and Mr. Smith's sincere satisfaction with the orthodontic results obtained for their daughter. All the while, the other parents were continuing, unabatedly, to read their magazines, watch the two tv monitors, or control their respective toddler. In a word, the other occupants in the room were oblivious to the conversation going on between Schachter and Mrs. Smith.

Then, like a bolt out of the blue, Elizabeth Smith, suddenly and shockingly, uttered the following horrific words to Dr. Harold Schachter: "Dr. Schachter," the woman's tone having turned from warmth, just seconds ago, to icy cold condemnation as she said, "Do you *really even remember* our Nancy? I bet you're like all the rest, once you're finished with these beautiful young girls!"

Schachter not only saw the change in her, immediately, he felt each pair of eyes from every other mother in the room, as they turned full focus upon him with the words now being spoken by Mrs. Smith. The pro-verbial "pin dropping on the floor" was not reality to this dumb-stricken orthodontist, as the woman continued.....

"Well, whether you remember her or not, **you are the man responsible for her pregnancy** and, at 19 years of age. Aren't you really as.....?"

The woman let her pause accent her accusation, her facial muscles had drawn tight around lips which now appeared pursed, even puffed out, as she fixed her gaze on this man who had simply come to extend his sincere solicitude and greeting to the boy's mother. The quiet in the room grew into deadly silence. Even the toddlers, usually making enough noise to sound like a tribe of Banshees on the warpath, were strangely silent and focused on their mother's faces, who, in turn, were all fixated on poor Harold Schachter.

"Whatever can you possibly mean, Mrs. Smith?" Schachter asked after recovering from the initial impact of her mortifying words.

"Oh, Dr. Schachter, you know you made our little

Nancy's smile so irresistible, it's no wonder she was grabbed up by that John Robards....her boyfriend.....and, now our soon to be son-in-law. Yep, she's going to have a baby this coming September. *You're the cause for sure....!*"

At least there was reprieve with the woman's explanatory words and smile, Harold thought to himself, as he noticed the growing smiles on the faces of the other mothers in the room who just moments earlier, had the nails ready for Mrs. Smith to use in her crucifixion of "an accused statutory rapist....!"

I'm sure Dr. Harold Schachter might have thought, on his drive home that evening, **'Well, it was all there, everything, except the girl's father, and the.....shotgun!'**

—Submitted by: Harold Schachter, D.D.S., M.S.
Schachter & Lang Orthodontic Assoc., P.A.
Ocean, NJ

"A
RESURRECTION"

The following report, from a Minnesota dentist, has happened to every dentist at one time or other. Usually, during a given day's work. This one had a ring of originality I thought worth sharing.

"I had a patient come in late for his appointment, not the first time for this guy I might point out. This time he really used an original excuse...."

"Sorry I'm late, Doc! I was in a *fatal auto accident with casualties.*"

—*Submitted by:* Nelson M. Hersh, D.D.S., M.S.
Shelby Twp., MN

210

"Mrs. King and Martha Ray"

*M*rs. King, a sweet lady in her 90's, was told by Dr. Barbara Pampalone that she needed some apical surgery around a bicuspid, in order to avoid extraction of the tooth. Apical surgery, or apicoectomy as it is oftentimes referred to in dental circles, is a procedure whereby the tip of the root is removed in order to resolve an area of chronic infection that prior treatment modalities have failed to eliminate.

"If at 88 you look and feel like you're 68, and you still have all your natural teeth as you do, I have to treat you as though you are 68. You really must go to the specialist I've referred you to and have the apical surgery done in order to preserve the tooth," Barbara argued.

Mrs. King did go, and all the teeth are still there. They do, however, require a scaling and prophylaxis (a cleaning) every three to four months. Last month, Mrs. King, no doubt growing tired of the repeated trips to the dental office for cleanings, looked up at Dr. Pampalone during the prophy procedure, grinned, and in an impish fashion said:

"Some 'Martha Ray's' would make things a lot easier....right now!"

—*Submitted by:* B.K. Pampalone, D.D.S.
Chatsworth, CA

"LEAVE 'EM IN A WHILE...."

The following story confirms we dentists never, certainly not, do anything without rhyme or reason.

At first, it might appear we have overlooked something, but, with our reassurance to the patient, it is quickly evident nothing is done without justification....of course not!

Dr. Stacy Colbert had experienced a long, arduous afternoon of dentistry. She was bone tired. Even so, there was one more patient to see, one with a lot of work to be done. And, as fate would have it after an exceptionally tough day, the patient requested Dr. Colbert to complete all his work at this appointment!

Tired as she was, Stacy agreed to go ahead and do as much of the work as humanly possible. After restoring eight teeth, mostly three-surface silver fillings, and a couple of two-surface composite restorations (white type fillings usually done in front teeth), a satisfied patient was dismissed by one exhausted dentist.

Even though the day had been long and physically draining, Dr. Colbert had to remain in the office for about an hour in order to complete some paper work. When the phone rang at 7 p.m., she was sorely tempted not to answer. However, being the conscientious dentist she is, Stacy picked the phone up....guess who? Yes, Bob, the last patient!

"Dr. Colbert, this is Bob Snyder."

"Oh, hi, Bob...." she responded, instantly thinking he wasn't calling to ask her out for dinner, but probably to report a filling had broken or, worse even, pain from one of the deep restorations she had placed. She didn't want to ask, but knew she had to get it out.... "Is everything okay?"

"Actually, I'm not sure, Doctor. You know those rolls of cotton you put in my mouth doing the fillings....?"

....Cotton rolls are used by the dentist to keep the tooth or teeth as dry as possible, while doing fillings. They are often placed between the cheeks, lips or the tongue and the teeth....depending on the area being worked on at the time. The rolls are about 2 to 2 1/2 inches long, and a dentist will often place one in each quadrant of a patient's mouth. This means there might be from one to three rolls at a given time, on the right or left side....

"Why, yes, Bob, of course...." she replied, in a tone not betraying any sign of anxious concern for what he might be about to tell her.

"Well, when I started to eat a little while ago, I noticed I was having trouble chewing. In fact, my wife had said a few minutes earlier, my lip looked puffy. I knew it wasn't the shot since the numbness had worn off, so I put my finger in my mouth and found the cotton rolls still there. I was just wondering if it's okay to take them out, or *did you want me to leave them in a while longer?*"

Dr. Colbert says she felt like a complete idiot as she listened to her patient's question. But, her response like any good dentist, assured her patient the rolls *were not* left in there without purpose....

"Oh, I'm so glad you phoned, Bob. Actually, I do need you to leave 'em in there a while, until....let's see, it's about 7:05 right now....why don't you leave them in until about 7:30. **That should give the material plenty of time to....to do what I wanted.**"

"Great, Dr. Colbert, no problem. I told my wife you must have wanted them to stay longer, or you'd have removed them at the office."

"Yeah....right, Bob. That's exactly right. Thanks again for calling."

Postscript: Of course the rolls had absolutely no usefulness, whatsoever, after the dental procedure was completed. Dr. Colbert's fatigue no doubt caused her to overlook them....nothing serious or life threatening, **not like leaving a hemostat in someone's chest cavity**, huh? But, important enough not to admit they were there for any reason, other than to give the dental work a better prognosis....certainly not!

—*Submitted by:* **Stacy Colbert, D.M.D.**
Pleasant Hills, PA

"DOK-TOR DAN'S BRIDGE...."

*T*his story, after the initial humor is extracted, is clearly a classic case for why dentists now spend so much of their time and energy on patient education, particularly on the home-care phase. The episode took place in Buffalo, N.Y., some 25 years ago.

Matthew E. Cohl was in orthodontic specialty training there, but was practicing general dentistry in the office of one of that city's general dentists. The practice was apparently quite large, with many dentists working there while they were in their various specialty training programs in Buffalo. The patient population was, in large part, of Eastern European origin. Most were immigrants or first generation Americans.

One evening, during the course of treating his schedule of patients, Dr. Cohl was introduced to a new patient, a former high ranking officer on the Buffalo police force. The man was 82 years old, but still stood tall and erect. He had a full head of thick brown hair

which he wore in a short crew cut. He looked every bit the formidable policeman, even at that advanced age. He indicated to Dr. Cohl, with his chief complaint, all his lower teeth were causing him severe pain, and his wife had been increasingly complaining about his breath.

Cohl's clinical examination disclosed a full upper denture, with a lower removable partial denture. The lower partial had at least six to eight metal clasps, maybe more. He simply recalls there seemed to be one on each of the old gentleman's remaining molars and bicuspids, thus making for a potential of at least eight of these metal attachments.

....A partial denture is usually understood to be a dental prosthesis which can be removed for cleaning purposes, at will, by the patient. Structurally, the framework is usually made of a very hard metal, like ticonium or chromium-cobalt steel, in combination with a processed plastic or resin, called acrylic. The latter holds the missing teeth in place.

....The partial is usually held in place by attaching it to the remaining natural teeth with something called a clasp attachment. This component of the partial is the retentive feature and can be made in a number of different shapes. One of the most common types is called a circumferential or c clasp, since it wraps around the patient's tooth like the letter c. These were the type of clasps holding this patient's partial in place.

The clinical evaluation also, unfortunately, allowed Matthew Cohl to see where the patient's pain and other problem was coming from....*each of the metal clasps was totally embedded in the teeth to which they were attached for retention.* There was an enormous area of decay above and below each of the metal arms. The decay was so severe, according to Dr. Cohl, he could not understand why the teeth had not fractured (visualize a tree, cut deeply around its entire trunk and you will have an analogy similar to this situation).

"Okay, please take out your lower partial, and let's see what we can do for your problem," Matthew said, as he silently wished for a face mask to help with the ex fetor oris (bad breath) coming from all those decayed teeth. Remember, these were the days before OSHA and AIDS, and dentists looking like space travelers instead of the "wet fingered" practitioners which most of us were 25 years ago.

The patient, in his broken and exasperated English, replied, "Vel, ya see, Dok-tor, dats da problem! Evar since old Dok-tor Dan gave da bridge to me three yars ago, I nevar for one time been able to take it out-a-my-mouth...."

Matthew Cohl says he immediately excused himself, went to the bathroom and rolled around on the floor for 20 minutes, laughing until he turned blue....a moment he has never forgotten!!

—*Submitted by:* Matthew E. Cohl, D.D.S.
Orthodontist
Plantation, FL

"A FOOL PROOF
DENTURE TEST...."

*D*r. Martin A. Brown had been in private practice a short while when he met a patient who introduced him to a unique way of testing the functional capability of a new set of dentures. A test, for her, which was absolutely conclusive in its ability to determine if a new set of dentures would benefit her eating efforts. A test, to Dr. Brown's knowledge, which had never been taught in any dental school prosthodontic course he was aware of (prosthodontics being a discipline the dental curriculum uses to teach students how to make false teeth).

The patient, an elderly female, had come to the office with a chief complaint stated as, "I need a new set of plates." Dr. Brown's clinical examination confirmed the patient's were ill-fitting, with the surfaces of the teeth being well worn. Brown, with his chest puffed up, assured her that he could make a set of teeth which would be an improvement over her existing "plates."

After receiving her consent to proceed, and then

actually treating the lady on multiple appointments thereafter, he found her to be a very sweet and cooperative denture patient. The final appointment arrived and his assistant seated the patient, in preparation for Dr. Brown's try-in and delivery of the completed denture. Martin placed the dentures, made some adjustments, and asked the woman to sit with them for a while in order to see how they felt in her mouth. He then left the room to give the patient some time alone.....

Upon returning to the operatory a little while later, Martin Brown noticed his patient, her back turned to him, her cheeks seemed to be ballooned and in rhythmic movement. Like any dentist who has just delivered a completed denture, and then finds the patient out of the chair when he returns to the operatory, he asked, hesitantly, if everything was okay. Her startled reply, though muffled and mumbled, actually garbled, was a "yes."

Just about the time Brown heard her "garbily gook" response, he also noted the pack of crackers in her hand. Now, he realized the cheek movements meant she was chewing.....and, after chewing a few more seconds, then swallowing, the patient perceived the quizzical look on the dentist's face required more than the simple "yes." She expanded with, **"Bout the only ways I can tell if new plates is gonna be suitable. It's a darn near fool proof test, you know."**

"And, do these pass your test?" Brown asked, almost bursting an artery to keep from laughing in the woman's face.

"Oh, Doctor, these are gonna be just fine. **They passed the cracker test!"**

—Submitted by: Martin A. Brown, D.D.S.
Fountain Hills, AZ

"OH, MY, THEY'RE SO, SO FEMININE...."

*T*his story, besides its inescapable humor, features the traits of imagination, resourcefulness, compassion, and concern, that Dr. Barbara Pampalone would not abandon for a down and out patient....

"Barb, dear, I was wondering if you would see a friend of mine?" a *social acquaintance* asked on the phone late one evening. "I'd take her to my dentist, but he's so expensive."

'Okay,' Barbara thought to herself, 'I'll believe she asked me to see her friend because my office is close to the school, and not because **I'm cheap**. She also made a mental note, when the friend mentioned *her Beverly Hills dentist*, to consider raising her own fees....

The gist of the call was centered around the acquaintance being told by the school district, to terminate "the friend" because the woman had not replaced a missing front tooth as she had been told. Since "the friend" was employed by Barbara's socialite acquaintance, she was trying to avoid firing her, a woman who was obviously unable to pay the Beverly Hill's dentist's fees.

"Sounds like she'll need a stayplate, a temporary-like denture, which will have the missing tooth on it. It'll cost about $200. I'll have my office make you an appointment for after lunch tomorrow," Barbara said, in acquiescence to the solicitation.

The socialite and "*her friend*" arrived at the office at 1 p.m. the next day. Barbara waved at *her acquaintance* through the business window, as she walked towards the operatory to assess the new patient's problem.

Clinically, it was not pretty nor the story very funny. Essentially, the patient, in her late 50's, was wearing a lower partial which had been patched about five years ago. The upper denture had been repaired so many times, with "store bought material," that each of the multiple cracks in the pink acrylic base had widened until there was enough space between the right front tooth, and the lateral incisor, that it looked like a tooth was missing....even though it really was not.

Two things worsened the situation. One, the patient's husband had been diagnosed with cancer five years ago, about the time the lower partial was patched, and had recently died, leaving her huge medical bills to pay off. Secondly, and alarming to Dr. Pampalone, was the tissue in the palate....it looked like hamburger and Barbara's thought, when she saw it, was 'I don't have a denture to make, I've got palatal cancer and it needs removing.....yesterday.'

"Where's your *can of goodies?*" Barbara asked her husband, a retired dentist and the office's resident "lab man."

"What do you need that for?" her husband asked, somewhat surprised by the request.

"I've got an unrepairable upper denture and need one of those we finished, but never delivered, or a used one that might help me perform a miracle."

Keep in mind, before the advent of AIDS, offices often kept old dentures and partials for the supply of teeth they provided when a patient came in with a missing tooth in their denture.

"I can repair any denture made by man!" her husband responded, with his usual modesty.

"Not this one, my love. Anyway, I've already told

the poor soul I'd search our lab for an old denture which might offer more promise than the thing she has in her mouth right now. She cannot afford a new one, and I must get this thing out of her mouth...today!"

With that, Barbara placed the patient's denture on the bench beside her husband. He looked at it, not saying a word, then pushed back his stool and headed for his secret treasure of "coffee can dentures." In a few minutes, he returned with a hand full of *prospects for a miracle*.

Immediately, she zeroed in on one that looked brand new. She picked it up, admiring the unexpected find, then quickly recalled, "Oh, I remember this one. I made it for that nice little Mexican lady who never came back for the completed denture. Oh, well, it's much too small! Too bad."

She studied several others, then, like a light bulb being turned on, her eyes brightened as she picked up an old, used denture that obviously struck some chord or notion in her brain that it would work....

Later, after piles of tissue conditioning (a material placed on the inside of a denture to treat the tissue for several months) and, the floor covered with a snowlike sprinkling of fine acrylic powder from repeated grinding on the old denture, the "bandage" was ready for seating in the patient's mouth.

"I never dreamed I'd stoop so low as to place a used denture, one discarded years ago, in this poor woman's mouth. While explaining the details of what I'd done, I handed her the mirror...." Barbara reminisced.

"Oh, my goodness, Doctor, my tongue.....It feels so good to my tongue!"

"I'd not thought of the roughness she must have been experiencing from the multiple, self-repaired cracks in that upper denture...."

"Oh, my, what beautiful teeth!" the patient said, seeing them reflected in the mirror for the first time since the herculean task was started an hour earlier. She beamed as she studied the teeth. Still, Barbara was nervous about taking her out to the reception room, where the *acquaintance* was patiently waiting.

"It's all I could do under the....please be patient until the tissue...."

"Oh, Barb," *the acquaintance* interrupted, **"they look so, so feminine**. And you did it so fast! Thank you so much!"

"Can you believe it worked? And they truly loved them!" Barbara said to her husband, as she returned to lab, and let out a sigh of relief.

"You're lying!"

"I swear, they absolutely adored the denture. I can't believe it myself!"

"Look, I remember that hairy bruiser. He reminded me of Spencer Tracy's character, Mr. Hyde. **He had a mouth the size of a gorilla**! I can't believe you did it. How could you?"

"A miracle, my love. **A miracle right out of your coffee can!**"

—*Submitted by:* B.R. Pampalone, D.D.S.
Chatsworth, CA

"But, it's not my problem...."

Dr. Andy Garrott, a former student of mine, is a guy who can get a laugh out of a confirmed cudmudgeon. Andy possesses a spirit of humor which is built into every fiber of his being. Perhaps it's the way he says things, or his facial expressions. I don't know....

"Joe, an *old* man came in the other day...old, like *ancient*. Okay? You got the picture?"

"Yeah, I got it Andy. Like Methuselah," I responded.

"Exactly! So old, the thick hair growing out of his ears looked like a pot of flowers."

"Right!" I quickly answered to keep Andy going, knowing he might slide off on a tangent.

"I go into the operatory, introduce myself, and ask him what the problem seems to be?"

"What'd you say?" the old man asked, his head tilted and, with a hand cupped over his ear.

"I said, *what seems to be the problem?*" Andy repeated.

"You're going to have to speak up, Doc, I'm a little hard of hearing."

"I SAID, *WHAT SEEMS TO BE YOUR PROBLEM?*" his voice now loud enough to bring the receptionist back to the operatory.....

"What's the problem, Dr. Garrott?" Patty asked, as Andy stared at her in disbelief.

"He could hear what you said?" Andy incredulously asked her.

"Oh, sure, I didn't have any trouble at all. Maybe you need to pronounce your words more distinctly. Let me know if you need me," Patty said with a smile.

'I didn't know anything was wrong with my diction,' Andy thought to himself.....

"*NOW, WHAT SEEMS TO BE THE PROBLEM?*" he again asked, paying attention to his pronunciation, and mouthing the words with great deliberation in the patient's face. His voice level now loud enough for people in the parking lot to pause, look around, and then cautiously walk toward the clinic's front door.

"Joe, about this time, the old guy reaches up and

pulls his hearing aids out, messes with one, incoherently mumbles something to himself, or no one in particular, then shouts..."

"Hell, Doc, these here hearing aids ain't got the batteries in....how bout making me some new plates?" he responded, his voice at least as loud as Andy's last attempt to determine what he wanted.

"Doctor Andy...." his receptionist said, as she walked up to him in the hallway just outside the operatory where Andy was now bent over, his hands covering his mouth..... **"You really should make an appointment to have your hearing checked. Patients have been coming in asking what all the shouting's about....!"**

—*Submitted by:* L.A. Garrott, D.M.D.
Batesville, MS

"THE CHAIRMAN'S FLYING TEETH"

For full appreciation of the humor in this story, it is necessary for the non-dentist, as well as graduates from dental schools after 1969, to first comprehend what dental education was like in those "pre-individual rights" days.

First, students were treated like **marine boot camp recruits**. I'm serious. Ask anyone who attended dental school in the '40s, '50s or '60s. There will be some variation, depending on the school and who made up the faculty, of course. However, one central core of truth will be heard from the dentists educated in those days....dental colleges were not concerned with individual rights, not like the decades which have followed. They were concerned with turning out an individual who was a professional in every sense of the word....from the manual dexterity skill level, to the code of dress and conduct. These were measured on a daily basis.

The second point I need to make before going on with the story, is the fact that everything a student did

in those days had to be as close to perfection as humanly possible. None of this stuff about "perhaps the student is functioning at his or her optimum level," or, "to expect more might be unrealistic." I was in dental school in the '60s and taught crown and fixed bridgework in the '70s and '80s, so I know of what I speak. I've been on both sides, the receiving and giving. Yesterday, the dental faculty was highly respected, sometimes revered for their technical skills. Today, faculty sometimes share brown bag lunches with the students, so as "not to be out of touch with their problems and concerns."

One last explanatory digression, and I'll get to the story. First, let me describe what study or diagnostic casts are....an essential element of this story. Briefly, they are stone reproductions of a patient's upper and lower teeth and some of the adjacent soft tissues. They can be textbook beauties, perfect, without bubble or void, glossy, smooth, exact manifestations of an individual's upper and lower arches. They can also look like a cow pile, if the person pouring the model is in a hurry, or doesn't care. Orthodontists and some other areas of dentistry, routinely rely on the first type. In my dental school days and those of the dentist who presented me with this story, perfect diagnostic casts were not just expected, they were demanded.

Yes, perfection was not just expected, it was required! And, even though we respected most of the faculty that demanded this of us, we also **hated them to the core**, at times. Most of us, with time, probably forgave and forgot real or imagined injuries to our pride and or ego, suffered under the tutelage of some of these prehistoric professors. But, sometimes, that anger would go on and on and.....

"Dear Dr. Portera,

Most of my dental experiences have been frustration, hard work, and gloom, but there has also been some self-accomplishments along the way."

God bless this man! What an honest soul. So much like many dentists I have known over the years, but unlike a lot of them, completely candid about how unbelievably tough and frustrating this profession can be at times.

He continued, "The happiest and most laughable time was when the head (chairman) of our orthodontic department almost went into cardiac arrest when I substituted some old study models (cow pod types, with enough holes and chips in them to look like they had been eaten by some stone eating moth, most likely), for his *prized genetic study models*. **I threw them across the room to a classmate and they hit the floor, breaking into thousands of pieces.....I hated him anyway!!!**"

What else can I say? How about forgiveness after 30 to 40 years, or respect for the faculty in the 'old days?'"

—*Submitted by:* Robert Griffith
Washington, D.C.

"ACTING LIKE A KID....!"

*D*r. Garrott, usually an extremely calm and easy going type of dentist, was attempting to work on a patient who apparently had a very high anxiety level. The dentistry to be done was really a minor, noninvasive sort of procedure, but, no matter how hard he tried, the patient's fear was creating a physical resistance that he couldn't seem to overcome.

After about 25 to 30 minutes of repeated verbal attempts at calming and reassurance, along with constant combating the patient's incessant arm and hand movements towards her mouth, this dentist had used his full tank of patience and was now running low on the reserve tank. The last of that was used when she coughed and sprayed him with saliva, as he tried to place the handpiece in her mouth....

"Mandy, I can't believe this. You're acting like a....like a kid!" Dr. Garrott said, in a tone of voice that was cracking with anger and, though he was still physically restrained, his face was reddening as beads of perspiration were beginning to build on his forehead and scalp. In a word, he was now mad!

"Look, stupid, I am a kid!!" the four year old looked up and said with righteous indignation and wild-eyed disbelief at her dentist....an adult who had obviously just lost all his perception of reality....

—*Submitted by:* L.A. Garrott, D.M.D.
Batesville, MS

"THE "DUKE" GETS DENTURES...."

*D*r. Arnold Weitenberner is recognized for his work on celebrities....

Yes, that is correct! Arnold personally told me about the time he was preparing to make a denture impression and, knowing how important the look and fit of the final denture depended on an accurate impression, he said to this patient:

"Listen, I really need a good impression from you today!"

Without missing a beat, his patient immediately responded to the instructions with:

"WELL, TELL YA WHAT, PILGRIM, IF YA DON'T GET IT RIGHT THE FIRST TIME, I'LL RIDE YA HIDE LIKE I OWN YA."

His patient, Carl B., drawled with the best impression he had of...yup, John Wayne, the duke himself....

Arnold and his staff simply broke up with laughter, after all, he did tell his patient to **"give him his best impression...."**

—*Submitted by:* Arnold Weitenberner, D.D.S.
Chesterfield, Twp., MI

"ONE MAN'S TEA IS ANOTHER'S POISON...."

A patient, having recently arrived in the U.S. from Pakistan, decided to take the advice of some of his countrymen, now living and working in America, and get his teeth cleaned before trying to find a job in his new home. He chose the office of Dr. Jeffrey Carrasquillo.

After taking x-rays, doing a clinical examination, and spending approximately one hour removing the dark, heavy brown stains which had come from chronic curry and betel nut use, Dr. Jeff dismissed his patient with pride. He had taken on, and consummately carried out, a cleaning and scaling which would have taken most hygienists at least two visits to do, at best, or *one they would have literally refused to do*. The teeth were actually bridged, or fused together, from the generalized build-up of stains and calculus.

Dr. Carrasquillo was so proud of his work that he suggested the patient take a look at his teeth in the rather large mirror in the reception room before leaving the office. He noticed the patient was making some peculiar movements with his tongue over his teeth, before leaving the operatory, but assumed it was natural for someone who probably had not felt the natural spaces between his teeth for years. He smiled and said good-bye to the patient, as he directed him toward the business office.

Jeffrey had just started to prepare a model for pouring in his laboratory when he heard a loud scream from the reception room area. Rushing out of the lab and running down the hallway toward the door which separated the reception room from the clinic itself, the door almost hit him square in the face.....as the patient from Pakistan burst through it, obviously on his way to making a hurried and unexpected return visit to tell the dentist.....with arms flailing the air and broken English going 90 to nothing....

"YOU HAVE RUINED MY TEETH! HOW CAN I EVER TASTE MY FOOD NOW? YOU EVEN ROBBED ME TO DO THIS....I'M NEVER COMING BACK TO THIS PLACE AGAIN!!!!!"

—*Submitted by:* **Jeffrey Carrasquillo, D.M.D. Elmhurst, N.Y.**

"GUESS WHO'S ON HER LIST....!"

The following is another story, paraphrased, but mostly in the inimitable words of Philip R. Jen Kin, which exposes a not uncommon type of patient seen by many dentists....if they've practiced long enough.

"A patient was referred by my brother who is a medical doctor. His specialty, no fooling, is psychiatry. The patient comes in and begins to cry about the condition of her mouth. She goes on and on, in her broken English, about the litany of treatment she has received over the years, and the dentists who have rendered that treatment. Most of the names I recognized as fellow faculty members or referring colleagues.

She brought a shopping bag into the operatory, literally, and proceeded to first withdraw from it a white cardboard poster upon which she placed all her broken and ill-fitting appliances....I saw bridges, crowns, extracted teeth and many acrylic night guards. She then proceeded with taking out a stack of x-rays, then followed this with copies of her dental records from all the past examinations. The stack of dental artifacts and records had to be three to four inches thick. Lastly, she took out three or four sets of orthodontic-type study casts and a handful of yellow stone models (not as smooth and perfect as the orthodontic type casts). I could hardly believe my eyes....I'd heard about patients like this, but this was my first one in the flesh!

The patient finished up her long presentation with a grand finale....**yes, she wanted me to testify against the handful of dentists she was presently suing**. Right, you guessed it, all I could ask myself was, 'Why me?' How in the hell was I going to get out of this fix? 'Pull yourself together, Phil,' I thought. 'You're a grown man, and you've got to get yourself out of this one!'

Now, I'm not stupid, but I have to admit I suffer from a hero's complex. I finally told her, "I'm not going to be your expert witness against these other dentists. I don't want to get involved, because I personally know most of the people you want to sue. However, I will help you, dentally, but nothing else!"

Yes, as the old dental adage goes, we got married. Not literally, but the type of union between patient and professional which causes the latter to see the former every month or two, for an adjustment of this or to fix that. Her bruxism (grinding and clenching of the teeth) has managed to systematically dismantle and destroy the work I've done thus far. She has continued to grind forward with her other lawsuits while our relationship, in my mind, seemed to be free of that type of threat. **She has appeared to have a genuine affection for me and my work**....then, the other day, my receptionist informed me someone needed to see me at the front desk...."

"Good morning, Dr. Jen Kin," the uniformed gentleman said with a *shit-eating grin*, **"I have a subpoena here for you to....."**

"Someone, please help me!!!!"

—*Submitted by:* **Philip R. Jen Kin, D.D.S.**
Cerritos, CA

"The genius of
George Bush...."

arry Switzer, having recently completed his two years of duty with the U.S.A.F., joined the private practice of an older practitioner, Dr. George Bush.

One morning, about two months after he had begun private practice with the older man, Dr. George walked into the office laboratory where Harry was doing some work of his own. It was readily apparent that the senior dentist was very upset.

"Damn, I've got to quit that laboratory....they're making me look terrible with this denture!" he said, as he threw an upper denture onto the lab counter top.

"What seems to be the problem with it, George?" Harry asked.

"I can't figure it out, Harry. I've adjusted and relieved the damn thing four or five times already, and it still won't fit Mrs. Adams' mouth like it ought to. This is the last frigging case I'm letting that commercial lab do for me!"

Just about the time the older practitioner's face was turning beat red with anger and frustration, Harry noticed another denture lying on the counter top with the name "Adams" written on the lab label.

"Dr. George, do you always make your patients two dentures?" Harry asked, quizzically, as he held up the denture he had noticed with the patient's name just mentioned by Dr. Bush.

"Why of course not! Only when I'm doing an *immediate denture*" (a denture made to insert on the same day a patient's teeth are removed). He'd just gotten the word *denture* out of his mouth when he noticed it....Bush literally snatched the denture out of the hand of the younger dentist, having recognized the mistake for what it was, and make a bee line toward the operatory where his patient was about to be delivered the *correct denture*.

Young Dr. Harry Switzer was near the front desk when the patient checked out.....

"Young man, if you become as good as Dr. George, you'll do quite well for yourself. Did you know he is a *true genius?* Why, when he tried my new denture in a little while ago, it hurt everywhere. ***It was like it wasn't even made for my mouth.*** Then Dr. George took it back to his own lab and in no time at all, he was back with my denture....which, I might add, feels as good as my own natural teeth. It's perfect! Now, you be sure and pay close attention to Dr. George! He can teach you so, so much, I'm quite positive!"

—*Submitted by:* **Harry Switzer, D.D.S.**
Phoenix, AZ

"OIL AND WATER...!"

A recalcitrant eight-year-old boy and a dentist do not customarily make for the best of buddies. This is an especially valid premise when the relationship is a forced one, like when a determined **mother demands the boy have his cavities filled, or he dies!** As anyone with half sense and one eye can comprehend, this would not make for an affable sense of togetherness between the two to be anticipated. The duet, not mother and son, but the dreading dentist and a belligerent boy who are about to meet in hell...the dental operatory.

Dr. Ronald Kunz said the boy was reluctant, recalcitrant, rudely resistant, and a number of other R words. Somehow, he had finally cajoled him into the dental chair for three fillings to be done. But, about the time he was to give him the injection of local anesthetic (the shot), Dr. Kunz had to excuse himself to take a phone call.

Normally, a patient is never left alone in the operatory, but, in this case, both Kunz and his assistant left the room. I haven't been told, from the "horse's mouth," why both of them were gone at the same time, so I'll exercise the right of my creative license...

Frankly, I think "little Johnny" was such a tyrannical little terror, neither of them could wait to get away from his evil little clutches, even for a few seconds. Okay, perhaps imagination on my part, but keep in mind I speak with a certain degree of authority...I have three daughters, the youngest being a five year old girl who somehow, but unknown to me, must be ingesting male testosterone. She can be a holy terror. Yes, I know this boy! **He became a mad-dog, on the loose, in the poor man's dental office**. It's that simple.

When Kunz and his assistant left the operatory, the rabid little urchin went into his blitzkrieg mode. They couldn't have been out of the room but a few minutes at the most, before he broke out of the chair. Actually, he made his break the very second they turned their backs to him. A kid like this one, you know, is a master escape artist. He's thinking major break-out action, when the rest of us are thinking how calm he's finally become. Oh, what serious judgment errors we make when dealing with these little devils! They hold master degrees in the science of escape and a Ph. D. in adult deception.

Anyway, while they were momentarily out of sight, he made a bee line for the reception room and, with lightning-like speed, drove his little paw down into the deepest recesses of his mother's huge satchel-like purse and came up with the keys to her new 420 SEL Mercedes. Now, I'm telling you it would have taken his mother at least five minutes, no exaggeration, to find those keys. He found them, and was out of the reception room door before the poor woman had time to ask why he was out of the chair. Her vocal cords were probably paralyzed, naturally, with the sight of him so soon after being carried back to the *"torture rack,"* as he was prone to describe the dental chair of Ron Kunz.

Yes, his break was clean. It was spontaneous and it was solidly successful. When Dr. Kunz, the assistant, and the wide-eyed mother stared out of the reception room windows, he was safely ensconced behind the wheel of the big black mercedes parked in front of the office building. All three of the spectators clearly saw the tongue, darting in and out at them like some hissing reptile, even the eyes had narrowed to such a degree they now appeared as two slits from that distance. He was definitely cornered, coiled, and ready to strike if approached

The next 15 minutes, according to my interpretation of the report, was a cacophony of human and sub-human sounds. There was horn blowing, mother's screams, cajolery and promises from the dentist, reptilian-like hisses and projectile spitting on the inside of the windshield and door glass, to name only a few of the strident sounds heard before **he was finally *recaptured and returned* to the confinement he cursed and swore, in the car he'd never re-enter...alive!**

—*Submitted by:* Ronald A. Kunz, D.M.D.
Pittsburgh, PA

"The Bulldog's gold"

As a dentist, I've had my share of humorous episodes. Maybe more! The account presented here, though humorous in a demented sort of way, is actually about the *most unusual request I've received as a dentist*. It was also, to my way of thinking, made by an individual who was temporarily out of touch, if not permanently deranged.

It was a Monday, just past noon, and I was alone in my office. This, as fate often arranges the field of play, was unusual. Normally, there would have been at least one assistant in the office, completing clean-up from the morning's work. Hell's bells, even the receptionist had left for a late run to the post office. Generally, she would have done this by 11 a.m., and been back in time to share lunch with me. But, on this particular noon break, nothing was normal....

"DOC-TOR...PORTERA! I heard my name called, loudly, and with a tone I knew was not bearing glad tidings. It was strident and anxiety laden. I sensed anxiety because the voice cracked between "Dr." and pronunciation of my name. It's hard to describe things like this, why you know what you felt. Anyway, I was in my private office, when I heard my name called, and it sounded like the individual was in my reception room, but moving in my direction. I got up, and started towards what I knew was going to be a confrontation, of some sort.

"Oh, hello Mary Alice...." I said, as I almost ran into her between the reception room and my private office. Her momentum, stiff body, red face and neck, enlarged eyes, set mouth and the arm which instantly started to lift her pointed and shaking right index finger in my face....as we almost collided...gave only one impression, indisputably, this woman was angry, to the point of hysterical rage. There was no possibility of my judgment being in error....

"You're the very cause, DOC-TOR...Portera! You caused it and you're going to get it back, so I can spend what that son-of-a-bitch spent to look pretty for his little honey! Do you understand, DOC-TOR?" She spit the words out like a machine gun firing bullets of frustrations and saliva. Each time she use "*DOCTOR,*" I heard contempt for the word itself, and for me.

"John had a slight drinking problem, I admit that, *DOC-TOR*.Portera, but he certainly wasn't a womanizer until you sold him on "cosmetically crowning his ugly teeth"...the ones that kept him out of trouble for years and, the ones I married 25 years ago."

Now, like a neon sign, it flashed across my mind...John Dorgan, a local businessman, had died last Saturday night. According to the rumor mill, he was in a Memphis motel with one of the young women he was purported to have recently been wining, dining and romancing, when he suddenly died of a heart attack in the "bluff city." His wife, apparently in a state of depressed anxiety, was now seeking answers to his infidelity and untimely demise. **I was the dog she was kicking at the moment....**

"Mary Alice," I broke in, "are you actually blaming me for John's death?"

"Maybe not outright, but I don't believe he'd been in a motel with that little slut secretary of Jake Dunstar's (a local attorney), if you hadn't made him so damn pretty. You know as well as I do, Dr. Portera, her voice now sad and resigned, John was dog ugly before he had all that gold and porcelain work done. Who, I ask, would've looked at a middle-aged man with a drinking problem and a mouth as ugly as his? Who, Dr. Portera?"

I almost reminded her she had obviously found him attractive enough to marry 25 years ago, but I knew the quip would only get me in deeper. So, I let it go, hoping my calmness might open the door for what she really wanted to say. At this point, I didn't know if she was here simply to vent steam, or make some kind of insane request for a refund of the money John had paid me for the reconstruction. I knew I had to tippy toe with her.

"Mary, I was so sorry to hear about John....I know it's tough! You probably didn't notice, but I did get by the funeral home Sunday night," I said, as I opened my arms in a gesture to hug her. She let me sort of half way hug her, but I could tell she wasn't there to be hugged, so I slowly and gently lowered my arms. "Is there anything I can do to help you and the boys get through this?" I asked, knowing the door was now open for her to toss the grenade in, or thank me and leave, having vented her anger with the man who "made a womanizer out of her husband," John.

"Yes, *DOC-TOR*.., I'll tell you what you can do!"

she said, with renewed contempt and anger after the lull in her rage. "You can give me the gold you put in my husband's mouth. I believe it cost $10,000. That should pay for his funeral and leave some for me to spend."

"What do you mean, give you the gold I put in his mouth?" I asked, with uncertainty.

"I mean I have informed the funeral home director not to bury John, until you have removed everyone of those gold crowns from his mouth. That's what I mean, *DOC-TOR...!*"

"You want me to go down to Lake and Barnes (the funeral home) and remove the crowns I put in his mouth?" I incredulously asked.

"Precisely! They're waiting on you at this very moment. You need to get it done within the hour, because he'll be in the cemetery in less that two hours. At least you don't have to *numb* his mouth this time, *DOC-TOR!*"

"Mary, you can't be serious..." I responded, in utter disbelief. "*You can't really expect* me to go there and extract that beautiful work out of a....out of my patient's mouth?"

"I certainly do expect you to do just that! You put that gold in, and you can take it out. If you hadn't done it in the first place, John might not have started thinking he was such a lady's man, and I might still have a husband. Now, you get whatever tools you need to do the job, and get on down there, or do I have to call my *attorney?*"

Oh, hell, now she had said it. She had said the word which strikes fear in the heart of anyone with the title Dr. An unspoken, implied thing had clearly become a distinctive, legal threat.

Like most professionals, the intial reaction to the voiced threat of a law suit becoming a real-life nightmare, is one of a racing heart and a sick feeling in the pit of the stomach.

It's probably a common feeling, when the innuendo is transformed by the spoken word, **LAWYER...a preying predator and, in this world, a DOCTOR'S most natural enemy.**

Yes, at first, I reacted like most professionals....then, in the seconds following her threat, I felt my own oncoming anger starting to build....

"Mary Alice, I'm really disappointed and hurt that you would feel like this. I understand and sympathize with what you and the boys are going through, but I have no intention of pulling the teeth out of a damn....out of John, so you can have a warped sense of punishment being fulfilled and perhaps sell the gold for...."

"So, you're not going to do it, huh?" she angrily asked..

"Absolutely not! It's ghoulish and a desecration to John's memory. If you want those crowns removed, you'd better get the undertaker to do it! I don't believe any of my colleagues do funeral home extractions....I can't think of one with the name, Dr. Frankenstein."

With my reply she whirled, tossed her head back and left in a huff, but not before saying, "Well, we'll see about this, *DOCTOR PORTERA!*" she said with a new measure of contempt.

My staff returned only minutes after she left, but I was so shaken by the incident, I was unable to describe what had just happened. In fact, it was close to a month before I divulged the extraordinary request from the widow of John Dorgan. The employee I told indicated it would have been hard to believe such an insane re-

quest, had she not seen John in the coffin....!

Having a healthy sense of survival, I had advised my staff we would close the office at 1:30 p.m., in order to pay our final respect to John Dorgan and his family. We, of course, had not originally planned this group visit to the funeral home. But, I reasoned Mary's anger might be abated somewhat, if she saw me and my entire staff paying our due respects, one last time....

We arrived at the funeral home just before the casket was closed. Out of deference to the family and my patient, I, along with my receptionist, walked over to have one last look at John. As we walked away from the casket, I noticed his widow had the *slightest hint of a smile on her face*....

Driving back to the office, one of the girls in the back seat asked, **"Doctor, did you notice those wrinkles around Mr. Dorgan's mouth. I swear, he looked 100 years old. I don't remember him looking that old...he reminded me of a *dead bulldog*! What do you think caused that, doctor?"**

I drove in silence....believe it or not!

—The author
Jackson, MS